M000009612

The Greenleaf Guide to
British Medieval Literature

By Cyndy Shearer

Copyright 2008, all rights reserved

ISBN 1-882514-45-9

Copyright Cyndy Shearer, 2008 – All Rights Reserved

Published by Greenleaf Press
3761 Hwy 109 North
Lebanon, TN 37087
www.greenleafpress.com

Table of Contents

Introduction

Material Covered in this Course:

This course is intended as an introduction to the Medieval British Literature. It is **NOT** the typical high school British Literature course. In a typical high school level literature scope and sequence, the study of medieval literature is included as a several-week-unit in a year long survey of British Literature that stretches from 500 A.D. through to the present. In such a course, students are generally given short excerpts from major representative works from each major literary period. There is little time to linger.

We are going to take a little more time. Our survey of British and American Literature will take three years.

This course, which follows a year-long study of Ancient Literature, is intended to be the first of three year-long high school courses on British and American Literature:

Year 1: Ancient Literature
Year 2: British Medieval Literature through approximately 1600
Year 3: British and American Literature 1600-1900
Year 4: British and American Literature of the 20th Century

Even moving at this leisurely rate, there is a lot of material to cover. The intent in this course is to give high school students representative texts from the period, and to give them whole texts whenever possible. If a student reads only excerpts, then they quite likely miss the full effect of the work, and the author's whole intent. We have resisted the temptation to increase the number of works studied by relying on excerpts. We've had to make some painful choices – and to **not** include the study of some important texts – but we're convinced that the omissions will be more than compensated for by a richer understanding of the selections which are studied in full.

For our study of Medieval Literature we will read the following:

Anglo-Saxon Literature-
> Bede, **The Ecclesiastical History of the**
> **English-Speaking People** (selections)
> Anglo Saxon short poems
> **Beowulf** (Rebsamen, translation)

Middle English Literature:
> **Sir Gawain and the Green Knight** (J.R.R. Tolkien's translation)
> **The Canterbury Tales**, Chaucer – **The Prologue, The Pardoner's**
> **Prologue and Tale** and **The Wife of Bath's Prologue and**
> **Tale**

Renaissance Literature:
> **Hamlet,** Shakespeare

World View Study
> **Rosencrantz and Guildenstern Are Dead!,** Tom Stoppard
> (a modern work based on Shakespeare's **Hamlet)**

At the end of this course we move into the English Renaissance for a study of Shakespeare's **Hamlet**. This will help students see the influence of the Saxon and Medieval authors on a later age. The course following this one (Year 3) covers the Renaissance period in more detail, including Shakespeare's sonnets, so there is some overlap between the two year's studies. But we do NOT cover any additional plays by Shakespeare in Year 3, so this is your one and only chance at a Shakespeare play.

The final section in the course is a chance for students to apply what they've learned to a work of modern literature which relies heavily on quotations from and allusions to the whole history of British literature.

You may note that there are only 23 lessons defined here – and you may immediately realize that most academic years run for 32 weeks. So what will we do with those extra weeks? If everything is running on schedule, then you could / should spend two of the 32 weeks on in-class examinations – to give students practice in taking a timed, scheduled test. You may also want to spend one or more weeks having students complete their own writing assignments on topics related to literature in the time period. And you may also want to spend more time on a particular selection, or add selections of your own. Those who would like to read more from this period might want to read all of Bede's **Ecclesiastical History**, all of the **Canterbury Tales**, more of Shakespeare's plays -- choosing more tragedies as well as his comedies and his history plays. In addition to that, I would also recommend Marlowe's *The Tragical History of Doctor Faustus*.

Vocabulary

At first glance, you may notice that many of the worksheets have significantly long lists of vocabulary words. The words are taken directly from the readings and are listed in order of their appearance in each particular reading. The best way to prepare for the vocabulary tests found in the SAT and ACT exams, is not to memorize lists of words in isolation, but to learn words as you run across them in your reading, and to learn them in the context of that reading.

Have your students read through the list with a highlighter in hand. Instruct them to highlight new words (or any words) whose meanings they aren't sure they know. Then, I recommend that the kids take advantage of websites like www.dictionary.com to look up the words (or you can do it the old-fashioned way with a dictionary). They should write these definitions down in their source books. Additionally, some students will want to make flash cards or set up a separate vocabulary file.

After the student has looked up the words and reviewed their meanings, students should read the assignment. If your student runs across a word in his or her reading that is unfamiliar, they should write the meaning of the word in the margin of their book next to the spot where it appears. They should understand the meaning of that word in the context of their reading.

Which brings me to....

Marking in Your Books:

I strongly encourage students to mark in their books whenever possible. If you are familiar with inductive Bible study methods that involve marking the text, this will probably be second nature to you.

Here are the kinds of things worth marking:
- Key words / repeated words / themes.
- Note speakers, changes in speakers,
- Write definitions of unfamiliar words / phrases
- Translations of foreign words/phrases
- Reader's own responses or questions to the text

Caveat: If do not own the book, DO NOT MARK IN IT!

Should you not be able to mark in the book for this or other reasons, I would encourage you to invest in a stack of sticky notes (ones with a light adhesive that will not damage the book – test these on a book with similar grade paper/type first!!!) and make notes there. Note cards will also work. Make your notes on these.

Marking in your book aids understanding in several ways.

- It makes it easier for students to find passages they might want to read/refer to in class discussion.

- It makes it easier for students to find passages they might want to cite in study or in writing.

- It makes it easier for students to follow themes/images that run through a short or a long work.

- It helps the student to focus on their reading and interact with the text at a deeper level. They tend to read more actively and are less likely to merely skim and/or lose their focus as they read.

Note to students:

As Daniel stood in the court of King Nebuchadnezzar, he was a captive in a foreign culture. Part of his **Leadership Training Program** was an extensive course in the *Literature and the Language of the Chaldeans*. Daniel 1:17-21 tells us that God gave Daniel and his friends "knowledge and skill in all learning and wisdom" (1:17) and that when they stood for their examination before the king, they outshined all others "in all matters of wisdom and understanding"(1:20). Because of his mastery of the literature of his culture, Daniel was able to communicate **Truth** to a very pagan King in a way that he could understand (see Daniel 4).

Most of the material you will read this year was written by men who shared a Christian worldview. They were intelligent, thoughtful people. Medieval does not equal primitive. Each work asks significant questions about faith, the nature of reality, death, sexuality, the purpose of life, religious expression and religious hypocrisy, courage, integrity, honor, and truth (just for starters).

These are questions that all of us want answered. They are also questions you will be called upon to answer at one point or another by friends, classmates, college professors, work associates and fellow church members. How do you know and how will you know that your answers are the right answers? What does God have to say to these questions?

If you know Jesus as Lord, you have been called to speak what Francis Schaeffer called "true Truth" to the foreign and often hostile culture that is our own. I would encourage you to see your high school studies as part of your preparation for the role that the Lord has called you to – to be his witness, and "always ready to give an answer for the hope that is within you.

<u>Finally, a note to parents</u>
who are using this Guide as a part of their student's home education program (either solo or as a part of a tutorial program):

AS MUCH AS IS HUMANLY POSSIBLE, please read the material along with your student. These readings will naturally generate discussion of important issues that you will want to have with your teens. It will be possible for some students to work through this study independently, but the study will be so much richer if you share in it with them. I would encourage you to see this course as more than a way for your child to snag a high school English credit.

As I noted in the "Note to Students" above:

Most of the material your students will read this year was written by men who shared a Christian worldview. All of it raises significant questions about faith, the nature of reality, death, sexuality, the purpose of life, religious expression and religious hypocrisy, courage, integrity, honor, truth. These are questions our children's peers, future classmates and dorm-mates, college professors, fellow workers, neighbors, and fellow church members will at one time or another ask them to answer. I would encourage you to see your student's literature study as preparation for those coming challenges.

Have fun! The material you are about to read is incredibly rich stuff. Drink deep!

   - Cyndy Shearer
    July, 2008

Bede's *Ecclesiastical History of the English Speaking People*

(You can find this text online at a number of websites. See http://www.fordham.edu/halsall/basis/bede-book1.html for one text. Penguin and Oxford World Classics also have print editions. All page numbers reference the Oxford University Press edition of *The Ecclesiastical History*. All vocabulary comes from that edition as well.)

A Little Historical Background

1. Read the following background information carefully, please. BEFORE you start reading Bede. Trust me, it will help.

Early English literature is generally divided into two basic periods – Old English, or Anglo-Saxon Period and a Middle English.

Old English / Middle English / Modern English

If you were to be dropped into the middle of Anglo-Saxon English (and had no knowledge of the German language) you would not understand much of the language you would hear. Old English has much in common with German because it was brought to England by invading Germanic tribes, notably the Angles and the Saxons.

After 1066, when William of Normandy conquered the Anglo-Saxon kingdoms, he brought his French-speaking Norman nobles with him. The heavy French influence changed the English language and English literature (in ways we will discuss later) from Old English to Middle English. But, if we dropped into the England during this period, you would still have a hard time understanding the language. It would be easier for you to pick it up, since many of the differences between Middle and Modern English are simple differences in pronunciation. Once you adjust your "ear" much of Middle English becomes intelligible.

By the time you get to what is referred to as Elizabethan English (the English spoken during the reign of Queen Elizabeth I in the late 1500's and early 1600's), the language would sound very familiar – especially if you frequently read from a King James version of the Bible.

The period you will study in this course begins around 500 A.D. or so and runs through the very early 1600's. George Bernard Shaw referred to this period between 500 and 1500 AD as "1000 years without a bath." Undoubtably, the combined effects of infrequent bathing and primitive sanitation systems could not have been pleasant. More popularly, though, it has been called "the Dark Ages," not because there were no candles, but because the barbarians who over-ran and conquered the Romans, could neither read nor write – and so kept no records. The Greeks and the Romans kept records; Alaric the Visigoth and Attila the Hun did not. What was preserved (often in monastery libraries) was likely to have been burned by illiterate Viking raiders, so many of the records that survived the Germanic invaders were later destroyed by the Vikings. It's a wonder we have any books from the ancient world at all. Contemporary records are scarce as well. As such, historians feel a little "in the dark" about what life in this period was like. Hence, the term: "Dark Ages."

More often, though, this time period is referred to as the "Middle Ages" because it is the period sandwiched between the "Ancient World" and the "Modern World." (The "modern" world the way Renaissance writers defined "modern.") It is typically used to describe the 1000 years between 500 AD and 1500 AD.

The student who is well-read in the Scriptures has something of an advantage in understanding the literature of this period.
The Venerable Bede, the Anglo-Saxon poets, the writer of Beowulf, Chaucer, and Shakespeare, all assumed that their readers would share a common understanding of the world – a common "worldview." They assumed certain things to be true about the world and the God who created it – and they knew that their audience assumed those things too. The fact that God created the world, that he was involved in the affairs of men and nations, that miracles happened, that prayer was necessary and the Bible true, was not debated, but assumed. That is not to say that all the writers of this period were believers in the way that most conservative Christians would describe it (i.e. that they actually had some personal and saving relationship with Jesus), but only that these were the things that the writers of the period generally assumed to be true about the world.

C.S. Lewis once commented that one of the benefits of conversion is that we understand the point of things that we otherwise would have missed. You may also find this to be true as you read this year.

SOME HISTORICAL BACKGROUND TO OLD ENGLISH LITERATURE:

Julius Caesar marched into Britain in about 50 B.C. and the Romans spent the next 500 years "civilizing" or at least "Romanizing" the "barbarians" they found there. As Christianity spread through Rome and beyond Rome in the first few centuries after Jesus' death and resurrection, it also spread to Roman Britain. There was a strong Christian, as well as Roman presence in Britain. Roman practice was to give land to army veterans when they retired – that land was often in the provinces conquered and governed by Rome. There were almost certainly settlements of retired Roman military veterans living in Britain. Perhaps even the centurion converted by Peter. And the native inhabitants (the celts or Britons) also adopted Roman culture. Many were also converted to Christianity. The areas outside of Roman control –

Scotland, Wales, and Ireland -- remained pagan. As long as Roman was there, these peoples pretty much left the Britons alone.

Around 500 AD, however, the world changed. Rome crumbled under the weight of its own decadence and the constant attacks of barbarian tribes. In about 500 AD, Rome pulled out of Britain. Those Britons who had joined the Roman army left with them – leaving the island undefended. Only the men too old or too young to fight remained. The Picts (from modern-day Scotland – that's to the north) and various other pagan tribes from the continent took advantage of the Roman departure. The Picts frequently painted their naked selves blue and came screaming down from the north, attacking the previously protected settlements.

This is the immediate background to your first reading from *The Ecclesiastical History of the British People*, written by a man we know as *the Venerable* Bede.

For a very good and quick biography of Bede, you should go to this internet site: http://www.bedesworld.co.uk/academic-bede.php. Here's a short recap: Bede was a monk at the monastery in Jarrow, who lived from 673 to 735. Most of what we know about life in early Britain comes from his writings. "Venerable" means something that is worthy of reverence, something that deserves respect, either because of its age or character of dignity. Thus, Bede was called "Venerable" not because his mother named him "The Venerable," but because he was much respected.

1. Now, before you go on to the first major reading assignment. Go read the information at the Bedesworld site, and answer the following questions.

In what year was *The Ecclesiastical History of the English People* completed?

Tell something of Bede's early life.

From the third paragraph of the article, list the things you learn about the following:

Bede's Scriptural commentaries:

His nature writing:

The usefulness of his exposition of the "Great Cycle of 532 years":

Tell what he wrote a textbook about. (Be able to explain what it was about, generally speaking.)

Tell a little about his death:

2. Now make sure that you can tell this wealth of information from memory.
    You never know when someone will want to quiz you on it.

Now, on to Bede -- *The Ecclesiastical History of the English People*

Vocabulary

In all the reading that you will do for this course make a habit of looking up words that you do not know and writing their definitions in the margins of your text. If you don't understand what the words you are reading mean, you won't understand what you are reading! In addition to that, the best way to prepare for the vocabulary sections of SAT and ACT tests is to build your vocabulary through reading and learning new words in the context of a passage of literature.

A word to the wise and all that (meaning if you are wise you'll look those words up). Those who ignore this wisdom, might be called fools by someone. I can't imagine who.

Make sure you can define and use each of these words:

> perusal
> unfeigned
> eschew
> ascertain
> impute

3. You will notice that Bede's *History* is divided into five books with a *Preface*. Read the "Preface," pages 3-5.

4. From the Preface, what can you tell about

The author:

The person he is writing to:

When this was written:

What he is writing about:

Why he is writing this:

The sources he uses:

5. Find the place (in the preface) where Bede explains what he sees as the value of studying history. Copy this section in your own handwriting below here.

6. Do you agree with Bede or not? Explain your well-reasoned answer.

7. Read Book I, Chapter 1, pages 9-12,
        and Chapters 13-16 on pages 25-29

8. Tell what you learn about the British people from this section. What are
        they up against, and how do they respond?

9. Read chapter 20, pages 33-34.

10. Tell the story of what is often called, "The Alleluia Battle."
(Write it from memory, in your own words, below.)

11. Read page chapters 22-26, pages 36-41. Then read chapters 32-34, pages 58-62.

12. As you finish this chapter, what are your impressions of this people as a whole?

13. How does the history (as told by Bede) compare with the history of Israel under the Judges or under the Kings?   Do you see any similarities? (If you have no idea because you don't remember anything about Israel under the Judges or the Kings....you have some research to do. Read the book of Judges, and skim through 1 and 2 Kings.   Then answer the question with thoughtful consideration and intelligence.)

14. Explain the significance of the following quotation from Book 1.

> *But when they died, a generation succeeded which knew nothing of all these troubles and was used only to the present state of peace.*

King Edwin

Background:

When we think of kings, we tend to imagine palaces and throne rooms where bowing attendants surround a monarch who is separated physically and socially from the common people. This model of monarchy came to England with the Norman king William I in 1066. The Anglo-Saxon kings were different. The Anglo-Saxons kings saw themselves more as fathers, protectors, and providers for their people. The king would surround himself with a council, his *thanes*. His thanes were his trusted warriors; they would fight for him, advise him, and support him. They expected the King to return their loyalty and trusted him to protect them and share his wealth (and whatever they might capture in battle) with them.

In addition to the king's thanes, you would find a Druid priest (or two) in the king's inner circle. The priest stood between the people and the gods and spirits. He was the spiritual advisor, a protector as well as healer.

Our knowledge of Anglo-Saxon religion is limited. The Anglo-Saxons have Teutonic roots and their religious understanding is rooted in Norse cosmology. Odin, sometimes called Woden, was one of their major deities. Human sacrifice was commonly practiced.

In this book, *Viking: Hammer From the North* (Orbis Publishing, London, UK. 1976) Magnus Magnusson cites medieval chronicle writer Adam of Bremen's description of human sacrifice practices about this time:

> *It is the custom moreover every nine years for a common festival of all the provinces of Sweden to be held at Uppsala. Kings and commoners one and all send their gifts to Uppsala, and what is more cruel than any punishment, even those who have accepted Christianity have to buy immunity from these ceremonies. The sacrifice is as follows: of every living creature they offer nine head, and with the blood of those it is the custom to placate the gods, but the bodies are hanged in a grove which is near the temple; so holy is that grove to the heathens that each tree in it is presumed to be divine by reason of the victim's death and putrefaction. There also are dogs and horses hanged along with men. One of the Christians told me that he had seen seventy-two bodies of various kinds hanging there, but the incantations which are usually sung at this kind of sacrifice are various and disgraceful, and so we had better say nothing about them.*

What few sources we have of the religion of the Germanic tribes (remember, they kept no written records of their own) contain descriptions of child sacrifice, the sacrifice of slaves, and occasional sacrifice of kings and warriors. If crops failed year after year, the people might begin with sacrifice of animals, followed the next year by sacrifice of slaves or prisoners of war, followed the next year by the king.

See the two pictures of the following pages of the Druid priest before his altar studded with skulls and of the Wicker Man.

The Druid priest was highly respected and feared (wonder why?) in the community. The king would have given him a place within the council and ignored him at his own peril. He was the religious leader, counselor, and healer. In Bede's account of Edwin, Cofi is the pagan priest.

Celtic religion—cult of the human head. Many Celtic tribes revered the human skull because they viewed it as the seat of the soul. By bearing away the skulls of their vanquished enemies after a battle and attaching them to their gates, they believed they were protecting the community by exerting con- trol over hostile forces. The divine power of the human head was enshrined at the Salwian sanctuary of Roquepertuse, with its niches for skulls surrounded by paintings of fish, foliage, and squatting gods or priests.

Illustration by A.G. Smith , published in **Life in Celtic Times**, Dover Publications, Inc.; Mineola, New York 1997

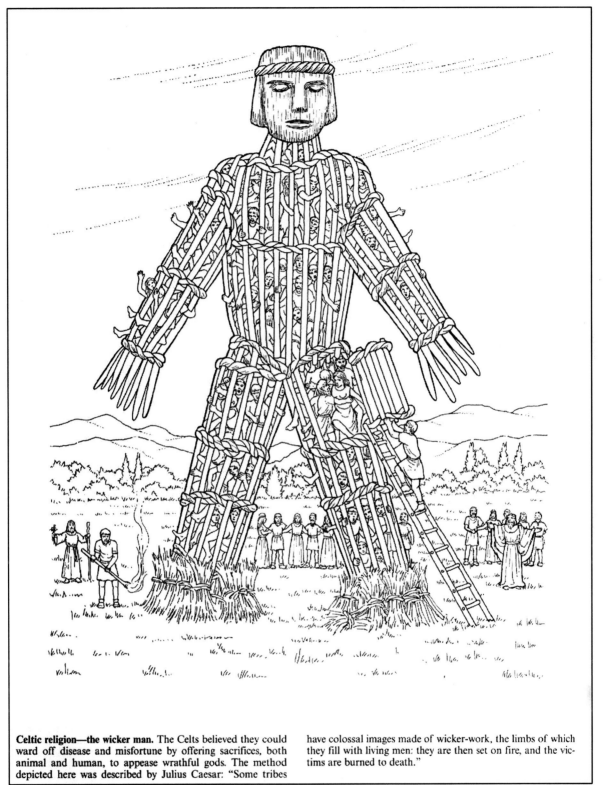

Celtic religion—the wicker man. The Celts believed they could ward off disease and misfortune by offering sacrifices, both animal and human, to appease wrathful gods. The method depicted here was described by Julius Caesar: "Some tribes have colossal images made of wicker-work, the limbs of which they fill with living men: they are then set on fire, and the victims are burned to death."

Illustration by A.G. Smith , published in <u>Life in Celtic Times</u>, Dover Publications, Inc.; Mineola, New York 1997

15. Read Book II, chapters 9-20 pages 84-107.

16. Tell about King Edwin. What is his background? What sort of man does he seem to have been?

17. Tell about Paulis' relationship with Edwin. What has Edwin's contact with the Gospel been up until their meeting? How does Edwin respond to the Gospel?

18. How is it that Paulis finally gets a hearing before Edwin and his council?

19. Tell about this meeting? What struck you about it? (If nothing struck you, read it until you are struck!)

20. Generally, how does the council respond?

21. Copy the reference to the sparrow and explain its meaning in the space below:

22. What sort of man is Cofi?

23. Tell who says these words, and tell why they are significant.

> *For a long time now I have realized that our religion is worthless: for the more diligently I sought the truth in our cult, the less I found it. Now I confess openly that the truth shines out clearly in this teaching which can bestow on us the gift of life, salvation, and eternal happiness.*

24. Tell what Cofi does. If you were filming this scene, how would you set the scene? What kind of music would play? What do his actions tell you about him? About the significance of the council's and the King's decision?

25. After Edwin's conversion, describe his reputation. What is Britain like under his reign?

26. From your reading so far, what kinds of ideals do the Briton's seem to have with regard to their kings? What character traits seem to be desired? How does Edwin model those character traits?

That's all for Lesson 1!

Anglo Saxon Poetry: the Shorter Poems

1. Read the following background information:

We are going to read two types of poetry from this Anglo-Saxon period of English Literature – several short *elegies* and other short poems, and one long heroic *epic* poem, *Beowulf*

An elegy is a sad or mournful poem or song. It may lament the death of a person, or it may lament what the writer sees as the sad state of things.

An epic poem on the other hand, is a long narrative poem written in very high, formal language that celebrates the heroic deeds of a legendary hero. Since epic poetry chiefly talks about the heroic deeds of heroic persons, to say that a poem is a "heroic epic" is a bit redundant. (So we won't say that anymore.)

Anglo-Saxon Poetry

When most people think about poetry, they usually expect to read something that is neatly set up in nice 4-line stanzas and rhymes. Anglo-Saxon poetry doesn't rhyme. Rhyming verse came into England with the Norman Conquest. Rhyme is a French thing, not an Anglo-Saxon thing. Anglo-Saxon uses very little rhyme and has no stanza structure. It has its own set of rules.

The Rules:

1. Each line is made up of two half-lines.

2. Between each of these half-lines you find a natural pause – called a *Caesura Pause*

3. Most often, sentences in Anglo-Saxon poetry do not end at the end of the line, and instead, often they will run from line to line, often ending at the half-line, so follow the punctuation marks carefully.

4. These half-lines are held together not by rhyme, but by alliteration of consonants or vowels. *Alliteration* refers to the repetition of consonant sounds. In this sentence, what examples of alliteration can you find?

    Beowulf bit a big bite of baloney

    Alliteration doesn't only refer to a repetition of initial consonant sounds. The sounds can appear at the beginning, in the middle, or at the end of a word.

    Alliteration usually refers to repetition of consonant sounds, though sometimes it will refer to the repetition of vowel sounds, though this is more specifically known as *assonance.* Notice it is the repetition of the vowel **sound** that makes it assonance, not the mere repetition of a particular vowel.

This sentence contains examples of assonance:

Nat and Nan attack the cat.

This sentence does not:

Nate draws Nan a car.

All the a's in the first sentence make the short /a/ sound. In the second sentence each *a* makes a different sound --   /ay/, /aw/, short /a/, and /ar/.

5. Anglo-Saxon poetry makes frequent use of something called **kennings.** The sea might be called a *whale-path.* Beowulf's enemy, Grendel, walks the *moor-path.* Hrothgar's hall is called a *gift-hall.* From these examples you can see that a kenning creates a word-picture by joining two nouns which modify each other.

It will be easiest to see how these techniques work as you read Rebsamen's translation of *Beowulf.* Rebsamen is one of the few translators of Anglo-Saxon who has tried to communicate not only the meaning of the original Anglo-Saxon, but also the poetics of Anglo-Saxon verse. In his introduction to his translation of *Beowulf*, Rebsamen described his goal for this translation: "I have tried in this translation to accomplish three things – to adhere strictly to the rules of alliteration, to imitate as closely as is practical the stress patterns of Old English half lines, and to choose Modern English words and compounds that give at least some idea of the strength and radiance of the original while also reflecting the tone of the poem." (*Beowulf*, Introduction, page xix)

In the translations you will read of the shorter poems, *Caedmon's Hymn, Deor, The Dream of the Rood, The Seafarer,* and *The Wanderer,* these elements are not as obvious.

For each of the short poems, I have given you a web address where you can listen to the short poems read in the Old English. The following websites also offer Old English language tutorials, in case you decide that you'd like to study the language in more depth. With a little work it is possible to develop a decent working knowledge of Old English.

Two good web sites with resources to teach yourself Old English are:

Wordhord: *Learning and Teaching Old English*
http://medievalstudies.uconn.edu/oeresources.htm

Old English Aerobics: http://faculty.virginia.edu/OldEnglish/OEA/

Now, with all that under your belt, on to the poems –

You can find alternative translations of these poems at this website:
http://www.tha-engliscan-gesithas.org.uk/readings/readings.html

2. Read "Deor's Lament" below (It may help you to read it out loud).

Deor's Lament

Weland, for a woman, learned to know exile,
that haughty earl bowed unto hardship,
had for companions sorrow and longing,
the winter's cold sting, woe upon woe,
what time Nithhad laid sore need on him,
Withering sinew-wounds! Ill-starred man!
That passed by, this may also

On Beadohilde bore not so heavily
her brother's death as the dule in her own heart
when she perceived, past shadow of doubt,
her maidenhood departed, and yet could nowise
clearly divine how it might be
That passed by, this may also.

Of Hild's fate we have heard from many.
Land-bereaved were the Geatish chieftains
so that sorrow left them sleepless.
That passed by, this may also.

Heard we likewise of Eormanrie's mind,
wolfishly tempered; widely he enthralled
the folk of the Goth-realm; he was a grim king.
Many a warrior sat locked in his sorrow,
waiting on woe; wished, how earnestly
the reign of that king might come to an end.
That passed by, this may also.

Now of myself, this will I say:
Erewhile I was Scop of the Heodenings,
dear to my lord. Deor my name was.
For many winters I knew good service;
gracious was my lord. But now Heorrenda,
by craft of his singing, succeeds to the landright
that Guardian of Men first gave unto me.
That passed by, this may also.

*-translation taken from **Twelve Centuries of Poetry and Prose: Volume Two**
by Alphonso Gerald Newcomer and Alice E. Andrews
Scott Foresman & Co., 1910*

3. Record your first impressions of the poem. Given that the poem makes references to people and events that are unfamiliar to you, you won't as yet fully understand it all. But what can you pick up from a first reading?

   Who is it about?

   What does the speaker's situation appear to be?

   What effect does the refrain have?

4. Now let's go through and find out what the original readers of the poem would have understood. For background information, go to the following link:

   http://www.anglo-saxons.net/hwaet/?do=get&type=text&id=Deor

   and read the notes on the poem at the bottom of the page

5. How does the additional background information change or add to your understanding of the poem?

6. Read *The Seafarer,* and then follow the link to an online text of *The Wanderer.*

The Seafarer

I can, myself, a true tale tell
I tell you of a journey – days of toil,
Times of hardship often suffered
Grim heart-sorrow endured
I have known a ship to be the home
of many cares and troubles.

Terrible waves rolling around me
as often I kept anxious night watch at its prow
when by the cliffs the boat was driven.
Feet fettered by frost -- bound by cold
while sorrow sighed hot around my heart
and inward hunger tore and cut .

I am sea-weary
The man who lives on land does not know,
He who happens to live most pleasantly on solid ground,
he does not know my wretchedness, my sorrow, ,
He cannot see the exile's footprint in the ice cold sea
where winter dwells

Bereft of beloved kinsman,
Icicles hang from my beard, ice crusts my clothes,
Hail stones fly. -- I hear no human laughter
only the roar of the sea.
Sometimes I hear the swan's song,
the gannet's or the curlew's cry – with these I pass the time.

The sea gulls' mew replaces meadhall songs.
Storms beat the craggy cliff,
From there the tern, icy feathered one, may sometimes answer
Often the eagle screams in reply
(frozen dew coats his wings)
No protecting kinsman to comforts my desolate heart

He who possesses life's delight, he who waits in the walled city
knows little of my grievous journey.
I must wait here -- In the sea path
in the darkening shadow. Snow falls from the north,
and hoar-frost grips the ground–
Coldest of grain- beats against me now
and I am humbled by this icy sea.

Yet still my spirit urges, and I test myself against the rolling waves.
My heart calls me far from here, to foreign homelands.
But in truth, search the earth and find no man so proud in spirit,
none so good, no youth so strong,
None so valiant, nor lord so gracious as to make this thing untrue –
Always sorrow will surround the one who journeys on the sea.
And always, he will wonder to what end the Lord will bring him

For him who sets out eagerly to sea - it is not about the harp,
the gold gift-rings, the delights of woman,
nor worldly pleasures, nor anything but the rolling of the waves,
and always he is longing,,

The groves bloom, they adorn the walled city
the fields be bright with flowers
The world hurries on –
But these only drive the eager spirit to the sea – to a distant voyage.
For him the cuckoo's sad and mournful voice –
summer's guardian sings of foreboding sorrow.
Bitter is his breast-hoard – the prosperous one does not know
the sorrows that await those who follows the exile's path

Even still, my spirit wanders wide,
my thoughts, to the sea-flood, turn again
Eager, ravenous and greedy, the solitary flyer
calls me back to the whale path –
and I am irresistibly drawn to the salt sea.

For I delight more in the Lord that in this dead life –
for life on earth is fleeting.
earthly riches can not stand.
One of three things will bring a man to his final day –
disease, old age or hostile sword -- uncertainties will come –.
All are fated to die – the spirit wrested away.

For a noble man, speak this about him after his death.
These are the best last words – speak of his good deeds on earth,
of violence against his enemies, of brave deeds against the devil,
and so his sons may afterwards praise him, now alive among angels,
blessed by eternal life, eternal joy with the band of noble warriors.

Here days of glory, all magnificence is departed from the kingdom of this world.
There are no more kings, no caesars like those of old –
no gold-gifting lords like those of long ago
when the greatest with him preformed glorious deeds.

Failed are the bands of warriors. Delight departed, only the degenerate remain.
The glorious brought low -- Earth's nobility grows old and withers.
So it is with every many who moves throughout this middle-earth.

Old age overtakes him, his face pales,
Grey-haired, he remembers his former lord, friends of earlier times,
noble children to the earth consigned.
Here the flesh no longer shields the body,
Here they no longer taste sweet things, nor feel bitter pain,
nor stir a hand, or think one thought.
Though the grave is strewn with gold,
and the brother and his kinsmen be laid beside him
with all he desires – The soul can use none of it.
Gold is no help before God's awful power.
Though while he lived here, he may have hidden it his fear.

Great is the Measurer's awful terror – because of it, the earth changes direction.
He established the foundation of the earth
the great expanse of its surface, the heavens high above,
Foolish is he who does not fear the Lord – death comes
to him unexpected and finds him   unprepared
Blessed is the man who humbly lives – to him the grace of heaven comes,
The Measurer establishes his spirit because he believes in His power.

To steer, one must have a strong mind, hold a strong immovable foundation
His word, trustworthy; his way pure.
To steer, each man moderation must maintain
desire the dear beloved, wish harm and hardship on his foe
Whether he wish fire for him, or that he be burned upon the funeral pyre.

Fate is hard. The Measurer is mightier than any man had thought.
Let us consider the home that is ours.
We then also strive – that we come into the eternal bliss
where we remain inseparable from His love, Bless is he
Honor to the Holy One in heaven,
There he is exalted, Glory Lord, Eternal God forever.

AMEN

- translation Cyndy Shearer

Go to a translation of **the Wanderer** here and read it (slowly) –
http://research.uvsc.edu/mcdonald/wanderweb/

7. Record your impressions of these poems. Who is the speaker in each poem? What concerns does each speaker have? What do you learn about life during this time? What Christian and/or pagan elements do you find here? Be specific. Does the speaker appear to be writing from a Christian or a pagan view of the world?

8. What did you like/dislike about the poems?

9. Read *Caedmon's Hymn*

Caedmon's Hymn

Now should we all praise   the Guardian of Heaven's Kingdom
His might   and His purpose,
The work   of the Father of Glory.
How He   of every wonder,
Eternal Lord   the Beginnings established
First He made   for the children of earth,
Heaven for a roof.   Holy Creator,
Then Middle-Earth, Mankind's Guardian,
Eternal Lord   Afterwards prepared
The earth for men,   Lord Almighty.

-translation by Cyndy Shearer.

Go to the following website for other translations of this poem:
http://oldpoetry.com/opoem/3852

10. Describe Caedmon's hymn. What does Caedmon write about here?
     What is significant to him?

11. How does understanding the story behind the poem's composition affect
     your understanding of the poem itself?

12. Read the poem again, out loud.

13. If you were reading it aloud in front of group, what tone would you use?
    What would you want your reading to communicate to the group?

14. What do you like/dislike about the poem?

15.Go to this website and listen to the poem being read in Old English:
    http://www.gutenberg.org/ebooks/19677

17. Read *The Dream of the Rood*

The Dream of the Rood

Lo! I will tell   the most wonderful dream
So it was   the middle of the night,
Long after men   had gone to bed.
It seemed   I saw   the choicest tree
led through the air,   circled with light.
Glorious cross   covered completely,
drenched with gold.   Precious stones stood
fair at its base   and five more studded
the shoulder-beam.   All the eternal Host of Heaven
beheld the Lord's angel there, This was no criminal's gallows,
but the holy spirits, and men throughout the earth,
each beheld this glorious work
This Tree of Victory, worthy of Wonder.
and I, outlawed by sin, wounded by its stain.
I beheld the Glory Tree   clothed with honor, shining with joy,
covered with gold.   Precious stones
adorned   the Lord's Tree.
Yet through that gold, I could tell
that it had already endured wretched suffering,
for blood flowed from its right side.   Stirred with sorrow,
frightened by that fair sight, I saw that eager beacon
change its garment and its colors; sometimes drenched with moisture,
sometimes washed with blood, sometimes with treasure covered.
I lay down a long while, and in sorrow beheld the Savior's Tree
Until I heard it speak:

The Best of the Forest spoke these words:
It was long ago, (but I still remember it)
I was cut off from my roots
Seized by strong foe-men
They made me into a spectacle, commanded me to raise their criminals
Warriors bore me on their shoulders, set me on a hill;
Many foemen fastened me there. Then I saw the Lord of Mankind
Rush with courage,   to climb onto me.
I did not dare to bend bow or burst
against the Lord's Word.   When I saw the earth tremble,
I might have killed them, but I stood fast.
The young Lord stripped Himself; that was God Almighty,
strong and resolute. He ascended the high gallows
Courageous in the sight of all,   when He determined to redeem mankind.
I trembled when the man embraced me, but I did not dare bend
or fall to the earth, I had to stand fast.
Cross was I raised.   I lifted the noble King high
Lord of the Heavens. I dared not lean
They drove dark nails through me. The wounds are still visible on me,
Open, angry, but I did not dare to injure even one of them.
They reviled us both together. I was drenched all over with blood
that poured from the man's side after He had sent his spirit
On that mountain, I suffered terrible things. I saw the Lord of Hosts
cruelly stretched out. Darkness covered
the Ruler's body   with clouds.
Shadow went forth with shining splendor, All creation wept,
bewailed the King's fall.   Christ was on cross.

Yet from afar, eager brave men came
to the Prince;   I saw all of that.
Afflicted with grievous sorrow, nevertheless I bowed
to give Him into their hands, humble and eager,
There they took Almighty God,
lifted him from His heavy torment. The warriors left me
covered with blood. With arrows cruelly pierced.
Limb-weary they laid Him, stood themselves at His head,
And there beheld the Heaven's Lord. He, for a while, rested,
weary after the great battle. In the sight of his killers,
the warriors began to build Him a sepulcher, carved from bright stone.
There they lay their Victorious Lord, and began to sing, sorrowful song
wretched in the twilight. . Weary, they wished after that to travel,
to leave their glorious king; There he rested alone.
Yet we wept there   a long while
Stood guard after the warriors voices
were gone.   His body grew cold,
fair body,   Then men began to fell us
all to earth.   That was a terrible fate!
They buried us in a deep pit.
Yet, the Lord's servants' friends heard of me,
Dressed me   gold and silver.
Now you can hear, my beloved warrior,
that I have endured   evil deeds,
grievous sorrows.   Now the time has come
when men,   far and wide
honor me, and all creation
prays to this sign. On me God's child
suffered for a while. And now, I rise high,
glorious under heaven and can heal
all those who fear me
Long ago, I became the cruelest of punishments,
most hated by men, before I cleared a way
of life for men.
Lo! The Lord of Heaven Guardian of Heaven's Kingdom,
honored me over all the trees of the forest,
Just as He, His mother also,
Almighty God for all man
honored Mary, herself, over all womankind.
Now, I command you, beloved Warrior,
that you tell all men what you have seen
Tell them this: On the cross of Glory
Almighty God   suffered
for mankind's   many sins
and Adam's   ancient deeds.
There He tasted death, but then arose
with His great might, mankind to help.
Into the heavens he ascended, and one day, hurries here
into this middle-earth, to find mankind
on Judgment Day. The Lord, Himself,
Almighty God, His angels with Him,
Will judge all men here in this momentary life
for He has the power to judge as they deserve.
No man will stand without fear
because of the word the Lord will speak.
In the presence of the multitude,. He will ask,
"Where is the man who, for the Lord's name,
will be willing to taste fierce and bitter death,

just as He did on the cross?
But they will be afraid then, unable to think
of what to Christ   they would begin to say.
No one needs to be afraid there, no one who bears
in his breast this best of signs
For through the Cross every soul from this earth
who intends to dwell with the Lord will seek the Kingdom,
who with the Lord intends to dwell
will seek the Kingdom

Then to the cross I prayed, glad heart,
great courage,   where I alone was
but a small troupe. My spirit
was driven forward;   endured such deep longing.
It is my life's hope that I, alone, may seek the Victory Tree
more than all men, and worship well.
My great desire is for such a heart. My Guardian is that Cross.
I do not have many powerful friends on earth,
for they have left the joys of this world, to seek the King of Glory
Now they dwell in Heaven with God the Father
living in Glory, and every day
I expect the Lord's cross, whom I saw once on earth before,
to take me from this transitory life
and bring me where there is great joy,
to rejoice in heaven where the Lord's folk
sit to banquet   where there is great merriment,
and set me there where I may afterwards
dwell in glory with all the saints,
and join that feast. To be my Lord's friend.
He, who here on earth,   suffered on that gallows-tree for mankind's sins.
He redeemed us and gave us life,
heavenly home.   Hope was restored
with glories and with bliss to those who had endured fire
when the Son, secure in victory, on that journey,
mighty and triumphant, came with the multitude,
host of spirits, into God's kingdom,
Almighty King, angels rejoicing,
and all the saints in Heaven, who already
lived in glory when their Lord came,
Almighty God, to where His homeland was

- translation by Cyndy Shearer

17.   Describe the first person who speaks in the poem. What can you tell
       about him?

18. Describe his dream, and then describe the one who speaks in his
       dream.

19. How is Christ portrayed?

20. From your reading of the poem, what qualities would you expect the Anglo-Saxon people to value in a hero?

21. In what ways does Christ exemplify (or fail to exemplify) those qualities?

22. Given what you have just read, how would you expect an Anglo-Saxon to paint Jesus? What would he be portrayed? What would he be doing?

23. What do you like or dislike about this poem?

Good work! Next week – BEOWULF!

INTRODUCTION TO *BEOWULF*

WORKSHEET 1

1. In this lesson, you are going to read about the historical background to *Beowulf*. You are also going to be introduced to the principal characters and Old English verse forms. Your source for much of this information will be the introduction to the Rebsamen translation of the poem (pages vii-xxi).

The introduction is full of pretty detailed information. If you are not used to reading this type of material, you may have trouble remembering what you have read. If that is the case, you will need to read slowly and keep a pen or pencil in your hand. Underline or circle important facts and make notes in the margins of you text as you read. If you just skim these pages, you won't remember what you've read. Taking notes will help you remember not only the general sense of the reading, but also the details.

So, TAKE NOTES AS YOU READ!

2. Read the second paragraph in *Historical Background* on pages x-xi to answer the following questions. (Refer to the map of Sweden and Denmark as you read.)

    a. The story told in *Beowulf* dates back to when?

    b. What is this period known as?

    c. Where did the Danes live?

    d. Find that place on a map.

e. Find the island of Zealand.

f. Who is the king of the Danes at the beginning of the poem?

g. Where did the Swedes live?

3. Read paragraph 4, page xi (in Historical Background), to answer these questions:

a. Who is the king of the Geats at the beginning of *Beowulf*?

b. How was *Beowulf* related to the king?

c. Who is the king at the end of the poem?

d. Who is *Beowulf's* father? What tribe did he come from?

e. What are Beowulf's wife and children named?

5. According to the section, *The Principal Characters* on page xi, how many characters actually speak in *Beowulf?*

6. List the names of the six important speakers named at the end of this paragraph and tell how many monsters Beowulf will face.

7. Read *Date of Composition and of the Manuscript,* paragraph one, page xiii to find the answers to these questions:

   a. When was the manuscript of Beowulf produced?

   b. In whose library was it preserved?

   c. How and when was the manuscript damaged?

   d. In 1787, what did Grimmer Torkelin do?

   e. As a result how much of the modern edition of the poem can be described as "sound," or true to the original?

8. Read paragraph three of the same section, pages xiii-xiv, to answer these questions:

   a. In earlier years, most scholars agreed that Beowulf was written during whose lifetime? (When did this person die?)

   b. Why do some other scholars think *Beowulf* was written in the eighth century?

9. Read paragraph one of *The Source and Importance of Beowulf,* page xiv-xvii, for the answers to these questions:

   a. Describe the view the paragraph says most people have of Anglo-Saxon England.

   b. Tell why that view is not accurate?

DONE!

Beowulf

Worksheet 2

1. As the introduction to the text says on page xi, there are "seventy-five personal names [that appear] in *Beowulf,* along with thirty-two names of places, families, nations, and swords." Of these, only ten speak. (In case you were wondering, the swords don't say much.) You should pay special attention to the six characters listed below:

Hrothgar – Danish king who built Heorot and whose kingdom is tormented by Grendel.

Unferth – Hrothgar's *thyle.* Challenges Beowulf when he stands before Hrothgar.

Hygelac – King of the Geats. Beowulf's uncle.

Wiglaf – Weohstan's son, young warrior who helps Beowulf kill the dragon. (OOPS! Does that give away the ending)

You will also meet two significant bady guys and one significantly ugly female villain:

Grendel – monster number one.

Grendel's mother – monster number two.

The Dragon – monster number three.

2. *AS YOU READ, DO THE FOLLOWING:*

- **Read with a pencil or a pen in your hand.**
- **Mark the text. Look for and mark any and all of the following:**

  Names of key people. Who are you reading about? Underline and circle the character's name the same way all the way through the poem. That will make it easy for you to keep track of the characters as you read. Notice how the character develops (or grows) through the course of the poem.

The beginning and the end points of speeches
made by main characters OR sections that
describe main characters.

Key places: WHAT is happening? Is it in Heorot?
In a slimy pond? Locate the setting and note (in
the margin) where each scene occurs.

Key events: Summarize the action described in each
section of the poem and give the section a short
title (heading). Write this heading in the margin
of your text.

Key words: Mark repeated or significant words or
phrases in the same way throughout the poem.
This will help you identify and follow key themes
of the poem and help you trace the development
of these themes throughout the poem. (Very
helpful to you should some evil person require
you to write an essay about your reading!)

3. Some questions to ask yourself as you read:

*Can Beowulf accurately be called the work of a Christian poet,
or were a few Christian elements thrown into a basically pagan
Norse story*?

Is the world of Beowulf *governed by impersonal Fate or a
personal God?*

**So that you will be able to take part in this discussion with your
usual cutting-edge wit and wisdom, here's how you should
study:**

As you read, mark every reference to *God* in some distinctive way.
Continue to do this all the way through the poem. (You might want to
mark each reference with a triangle, a cross, etc) Then draw the
same symbol in the margin beside the line where you find the
reference.

In addition to marking *God*, also mark the words *"wyrd"* and *"fate"* in
a distinctive way.

4. The Germanic religion had a fatalistic view of life. Whatever the gods wanted to do to me, they would do. Any attempt to change your fate, or exercise control over it was futile. The gods were impersonal and oblivious to your feelings and your circumstances. Your fate was pre-determined (what else would it be?) and there is nothing you can do to change it. Whining will get you nowhere. (I take that back, it might get you tossed out of the boat in the middle of the North Sea somewhere. Not at all balmy.)

But enough introduction.

5. As the poem opens, the Danish people are mourning their lost king. Suddenly, a boat containing an infant floats up to their shores. Scyld Scefing arrives. His arrival is interpreted as a sign that he has been sent to them form the gods. They make him their king.

6. Read lines 2-19.
7. Tell what you learn about Scyld from this section.

8. Read lines 20-26.
9. What do you learn about Beaw? Write a brief summary of this section in the margin of your book.

10. Read lines 27-52.
11. Tell what is described in these lines. Write a brief summary of this section in this margin of your book.

12. Read lines 53-63.
13. Fill out the genealogical chart below so that you can make sure you understand the relationship between these characters so far:

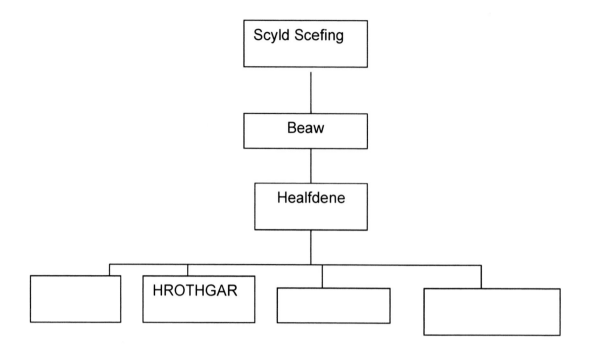

14. Read lines 64-84.
15. WHO are these lines about?

16. List the things you learn about this person.

17. Read lines 85-170. Who do these lines describe?

18. List the things you learn about this person.

19. Read lines 170-193.
20. Describe the effect Grendel's attacks have had on the Danes.

21. Read lines 1-170 again. This time make sure to mark all references to God. On the chart titled, "References to God" (Catchy title, huh?) record the words used to describe God and the names ascribed to God. Also indicate line numbers for each reference. Include every reference and its line number even where there are repetitions.

22. As you have learned already, **kennings** are a poetic device commonly found in Anglo-Saxon poetry. Explain what a kenning is (and give an example) below.

23. Find five examples of kennings in this section and list them. Remember that kennings are not always hyphenated.

24. Remember – Hygelac is king of the Geats. Who is Hygelac's thane?

25. Read lines 194-215.
26. What action is described in these lines?

27. Describe Beowulf's reputation among the rulers of the Geats.

28. What request does Beowulf make of them and how do they respond?

29. Read lines 216-228.

30. What action or event do these lines describe?

31. Read lines 229-267.

32. How does the "warden of the shores" greet Beowulf and his men?

33. Read lines 268-285.

34. Who speaks in these lines?

    What do you learn about the speaker's purpose for being there?

    What do you learn about his character?

35. Read lines 286-319.

36. How does the one who guards the coast react to word of Beowulf's intended mission?

37. Read lines 320-404.

38. Who is Wulfgar?

    How does he receive Beowulf and his men?

39. Read lines 405-455.

40. Who speaks here?

41. What credentials does he have for this battle? What are his qualifications?

42. How does he plan to battle the monster?

43. Who or what does he say will determine his fate?

44. What gift does he ask of Hrothgar if the monster kills him?

45. Remember to continue marking references to both God and to Fate. Remember to add each reference to your chart.

46. Read lines 456-472.

47. What previous dealings has Hrothgar had with Beowulf's family?

48. Read lines 473-498.

49. How does Hrothgar describe his problem to Beowulf?

    Given what you have read about a Lord's relationship to his thanes and to his people in general, why is the monster's continued attack especially significant (and troubling) to Hrothgar?

50. Continue to mark all references to God and Fate. What does Hrothgar have to say about God's or wyrd's role in this situation?

51. Describe the scene at the end of this section. If it were a movie or a painting, what would you expect to see?

52. Read the information found between lines 498 and 498 on page 17, then read lines 528-529.

    Who is Unferth? What is his position in Hrothgar's hall?

    Why does the poem say Beowulf's "boasting of sea-strength burned in Unferth's heart"? What do you think he challenges Beowulf?

53. Read lines 549-606.

54. How does Beowulf answer Unferth's challenge? Describe the specific insult give in lines 581 and following.

55. Read lines 607-701.

    How does Hrothgar respond to Beowulf's promises?

    How does Wealththeow respond?

56. Look again at lines 677-687. Describe Beowulf's plan of attack. Why does he plan to fight this way? What does that tell us about the kind of man Beowulf is?

57. What is the mood at the end of this section (ending with line 701)?

58. Continue to mark all references to God and Fate and add each of these to your chart.

Good work! Treat yourself to something fun, O most excellent student-type!

LESSON 5

Beowulf
Worksheet 3

1. Vocabulary

fen
mere (n. as in "turned back from the mere")
loathsome
vanquish(ed)
womb-seed (what would this be?)
booty (as defined in the dictionary and used in Beowulf, please)
gore
shambling
ipelled
hoisted
guile
hoard
ravage(d)
bereft
citadel
shorn

2. Read lines 702-863 (on pages 23-28).
3. Now that you have read through the whole section, I'm going to ask you to look more closely at the details. In lines 702-705, what consonant sound is most prominent? Tell what effect that has in terms of the mood that is established in these lines?

4. Do you find other places in this section where the alliteration supports the action described. (For instance, what kinds of actions would fit with the hard consonant sounds like /k/? List any that you find.

5. Describe Grendel. (Cheerful fellow that he is!)

6. Describe the battle between Beowulf and Grendel. What poetic devices add to the sense of the scene? (ex. sounds of the words, kennings, general descriptive images?)

7. What part does the poet say God plays in all this mayhem? List some of the ways in which God and/or Fate are described. Make sure you add these references to your chart.

8. How does the poet describe Grendel's water-"side" home? What mood is established by his description?

9. Do you feel any sympathy for Grendel? Explain your answer.

10. HEY HO! THE MONSTER'S DEAD! Put yourself in the Dane's position. The fear is gone, and the monster is dead. What would you most likely do next?

    Somewhere in your short list of things to do after Grendel is dead should be to **celebrate!** And that is what this next section will deal with. Unferth begins with a song that praises Beowulf....at first. He then goes on to praise Siegmund, the dragon-slayer, a legendary Danish hero. So read carefully, and don't get confused about which hero Unferth is describing.

11. Read lines 864-915 for Unferth's song. Then read lines 916-990. These lines describe Beowulf's triumphant return.

12. Hrothgar speaks in lines 928-956. Who does he thank for the victory? What does he promise Beowulf?

13. Beowulf answers in lines 957-979. How does he answer? What does his answer reveal about his character?

14. How do Unferth and the others respond in lines 980-990? What is so significant about Unferth's silence?

15. You just finished reading 980-990. How did the poet leave you feeling at the end of this passage? Another way to ask this question is -- what is the *mood* at the end of this section? How does the writer create this mood? Again, pay close attention to the sounds of the words, the images he uses, the actions of the characters (to name a few things). These elements should factor into your answer.

16. Read lines 990-1062. Clean up for the big celebration involves what kinds of activities?

17. What gifts does Beowulf receive? What is your impression of Hrothgar? What kind of king/man does he seem to be?

18. What references to deity do you find in this passage?

19. What are *loan days*?

20. In lines 1063-1159, Hrothgar's minstrel sings a song about a battle between the Danes and the Frisians. The translator summarized this story for you on pages 34 and 35 above his translation of the song. The song ends in 1159 when it says, "The song ended." (See, it's not so hard....)

21. Why do you think the minstrel chooses to tell this story at this point?

22. Read lines 1160-1191. What does Wealhtheow remind Hrothulf of?

23. Read lines 1192-1250. There are some obscure references to things that we don't know so much about in this section. Be sure and read the translator's explanation on page 39, before you wade into the obscure passages alone. (You should know by now, that wading alone in Beowulf's world can be dangerous.)

24. In this section Wealhtheow turns her attention to Beowulf. Be sure to read your editor's explanation of the gold necklace (page 39).

25. What is significant about her gift to Beowulf here?

26. What does Wealhtheow ask of Beowulf? Why do you think she asks this?

27. After Wealhtheow sits down, what do the guys do next?

28. What hints are there in this passage that all is not well? (The music starts building here....) To quote from Tom Stoppard's play *Rosencrantz and Guildenstern Are Dead!*, "There is an art to the building of suspense."

If you skipped the vocabulary study....go back and do that now, dear.

LESSON 6

BEOWULF
Worksheet 4

1. Vocabulary:

loins
wield(er)
helm
spawn(ed)
moldering
forfeited
roiling
tokens (not coins used in video games, please.)

2. Read lines 1251-1931 found on pages 41-61.

3. Read lines 1251-1259 aloud again SLOWLY. What sounds are repeated the most in the first two lines? What effect does that repetition have on the mood as part II opens?

4. How are Grendel and his mama described in lines 1262-1287?

5. Compare her attack on the sleeping warriors with her son's attack.

6. Where was Beowulf during all this fuss? How much of his foot does he stick in his mouth when he appears before Hrothgar the next morning?

7. What else do you learn about Grendel and his mother in lines 1345 and following?

8. If you were going to make a movie out of this section of *Beowulf*, what reaction would you want the viewers to have as they watched the scene described in lines 1420-1441? What would they see?

9. What gesture of friendship does Unferth make to Beowulf as they stand by the water?   How is that gesture received by Beowulf?

10. Think about Beowulf's response to Unferth (question #9) and his last words before diving into the water. What do these things tell you about Beowulf's character?

11. Describe his underwater battle. (Did you find that your reading speed increased as you read this section?)

12. How heavy was Grendel's head, by the way?

13. Describe Beowulf's return to Hrothgar.

14. How does Beowulf recount his victory? What does this tell you about his character?

15. What wise mindthoughts does Hrothgar, son of Healfdene, share with Beowulf? What advice does he give him? Whose examples should he follow and whose examples should he eschew?

16. How does Hrothgar describe Beowulf starting with line 1840 (and following)?

    What does his praise add to your understanding of Beowulf's character?

17. How is Beowulf's homecoming described?

Okay, two foes down......one to go.

LESSON 7

BEOWULF

Worksheet #5

1. Vocabulary

    pilfer

    to well (v. as in line 2139…"welled with gore")

    fallow

    acclaim

    renown

2. Pick up your reading with line 1963 and stop at line 2199.

3. Below are segment divisions for lines 1963-2199. Give titles to each segment that describe the main thing talked about in that segment.

    1963-1970A:

    1970B-1980A:

    1980B-1998:

    1999-2029A:

    2029B-2069A:

    2069B-2142:

    2143-2176:

    2177-2199:

4. Just for the fun of it, name the two warriors that were crunched and munched by Grendel and his mama. (Beowulf told Hygelac their names.)

5. What did Beowulf do with the gifts Hrothgar gave him?

   What did Beowulf do with the gifts Hrothgar gave him?

   What did he do with the gold neck-ring?

6. What gift did Hygelac give to Beowulf?

7. Vocabulary:

   unwary

   barrow

   burnish

   wane (waning)

   mound

   wretch

   byrnies

8. Read lines 2200-2323. Describe what is described in the these lines.

9. Read lines 2324-2354A.

10. After Beowulf heard of the dragon's attack, what was his first thought?

11. How does Beowulf plan to attack the dragon?   What does he NOT want to do?

12. In lines 2354B-2397A Beowulf things back over the events that led to his being named King. Tell how he came to occupy the throne.

Lines 2354B-2368:

Lines 2369-2379A:

Lines 2379B-2390:

Lines 2391-2397A:

13. At line 2397B, the poet has finished with the past, and picks up the story as Beowulf marches off to fight the dragon. How does he march? How many warriors? Who else goes with them?

14. Tell about the thirteenth member of the company. Why is he there? What is his history?

15. In Line 2417, Beowulf sits by the Cliffside. Read lines 2417-2424. What does this "keeper of the Geats" think about?

16. Beginning in line 2425 and continuing through 2510, Beowulf addresses his companions. He tells more of his life story. Read through this carefully to discover details about Beowulf's early past. What do you learn about him in line 2425?

17. Who are these people?

    Hrethel of the Geats

    Herebeald

    Haethcyn

Hygelac

What does Haethcyn do to Herebeald?

How does Hrethel react?

When Hrethel died, who became king then?

18. What is the trouble that is described in lines 2472-2489?

19. Who died in that battle? Who became king next?

20. After describing his service to King Hygelac in lines 2497-2509, Beowulf says, "and still I am ready while this sword endures/this treasured Naegling." What is he ready to do with this same sword?

21. From line 2490 through line 2537, we have the speech Beowulf gives to his men before he goes into battle. How does he plan to fight the dragon?

22. Read lines 2538-2820.

23. How does Beowulf attract the dragons' attention?

24. And how does the dragon respond? (through 2595)

25. How does the poet say his men rushed to his defense? (2596-2599a)

26. Who was the exception to this among his companions? What does he
      do?

27. How is Beowulf wounded?

28. What is Wiglaf a model of? (Yes, I know, I ended the question with a preposition…..)

29. What request does Beowulf make of Wiglaf? What does he want to see?

30. What do Beowulf's last words tell about his character?

31. Read lines 2821-3180

32. What do the people fear will happen after Beowulf's death?

33. What happens to the dragon's treasure? Why?

34. Read lines 3170-3138 again. How is Beowulf eulogized?

35. An epic hero is a figure whose life and behavior embody the values of his people. In what ways does Beowulf embody the values of his people? List specific examples from the poem. Then summarize your findings in either a well-reasoned paragraph or a short paper.

DONE!

LESSON 8

GAWAIN AND THE GREEN KNIGHT

Worksheet 1

While *Beowulf* is considered to be a work of Anglo Saxon literature, and was written in Old English, *Sir Gawain* is a work of the Middle English Period. (**KNOW THIS!**).

The Anglo-Saxon period in England ended in 1066 when William, Duke of Normandy (that's in what we now call France) seized the English throne by defeating the Saxon King Harold at Hastings (hence the battle is known as *the Battle of Hastings*. Clever, no?) With the Normans, came serious French influence – which had a significant effect on Saxon culture and on the English language. The Norman rulers were French and spoke French. They did not have any desire or feel any moral obligation to learn to speak the barbaric language of their conquered subjects. They spoke the <u>civilized</u> tongue (French, of course). As a result, what we now call Old English changed drastically. We refer to the post-Conquest English language as *Middle English*. You will learn more about Middle English as we read Chaucer. (Please contain your excitement, you won't have to wait long!)

Gawain and the Green Knight was written in Middle English. More specifically, it was written during what has been called the "Alliterative Revival." As you know from your study of Beowulf, Anglo-Saxon poetry did not rhyme, but was alliterative. As the Norman influence grew in the language, alliterative verse fell out of style. Alliteration was out, rhyme was in. But the writer of *Gawain* adds alliteration and what Tolkein calls "native rhythm" back, combining alliteration and rhyme, and using some innovative meter, as well.

Though Gawain and Canterbury Tales were written at about the same time, there are differences in the Middle English used in each work. Because of regional differences, the Middle English that was used by *Gawain's* writer differs from the language that those who lived in London would have used. That is why the Middle English of Chaucer's works differs from the Middle English of *Gawain*.

A Note on Pronunciation: Gawain does not have a twin brother named, "DUH-Wayne. His name is not GUH-Wayne. DUH-Wayne and GUH-Wayne would have mullets. This Gawain's name is pronounced GAH-win or GAW-win. Gawain does not have a mullet.

AND PLEASE NOTE: In addition to actually reading the first chapter/book of the poem, this week's assignment includes vocabulary to learn, a poem to memorize, and a news story to write. Use your time wisely this week ("And get some rest. Remember, if you haven't got your health, you haven't got anything.")

1. With that in mind, read the first paragraph on page 1 of your text, and then answer the following insightful questions.
   a. Name the four poems found in the manuscript that contains *Gawain and the Green Knight.*

   b. What date is found on the manuscript?

2. Now read the second paragraph beginning on page 1 and continuing to the top of page 2. Tell what we can gather about the writer of the poem.

3. The introduction goes on to explain that the writer of *Gawain* was almost certainly a contemporary of Chaucer, the writer of *The Canterbury Tales.* (You get to read *Canterbury Tales* next.)

4. Before you begin reading this poem, you have another poem to memorize. Don't neglect this. It will be on your next quiz. It will be a major part of this grading period's grade.

   Willy, Willy, Harry, Stee
   Harry, Dick John, Harry 3,
   1, 2, 3 Neds, Richard 2,
   Harry 4, 5, 6, then who?
   Edward 4, 5, Dick the Bad,
   Harrys twain and Ned the Lad
   Mary, Bessy, James the Vain,
   Charlie, Charlie, James again.

   William and Mary, Ann Gloria
   4 Georges, William, Victoria

Gawain's writer and Chaucer were writing during the reign of Richard the Second (that's Richard 2 in the poem.)

5. *Gawain and the Green Knight* is divided into 4 chapters, or books. This week you are going to read the first book. Before you read, look in the table of contents and tell me where you will find the "Glossary." Then tell me what a *glossary* is. Why would knowing this be helpful? (This question is not rhetorical, which is to say, ANSWER this question below, please dear.)

6. Vocabulary:

   (www.dictionary.com will be helpful for most of these, but some, marked with a * will only be found in the glossary in your book. Hint.)

   dainties
   dais
   appraise
   keen
   portals
   gorge (as in "his gorge")
   paunch
   *poitrel
   *crupper
   *molains
   *capadoce
   * pisane
   hauberk
   *haft
   vie
   *guisarm
   loth
   *cavil

7. Read the first chapter, pages 19-34. As you finish reading each section, briefly summarize the main event or events described in it. Name the main characters mentioned, and tell what happens or what is described, and write your answers on the chart on the next page.

Stanza	Who?	What?
1		
2		
3		
4		
5		
6		
7		
8		
9		
10		
11		
12		
13		
14		
15		
16		
17		
18		
19		
20		
21		

8. What is your general impression of the following characters:

King Arthur:

Guinevere:

Gawain

The Green Knight

9. List some of the people and events mentioned in the first stanza.

10. Why would the poet begin his tale about Camelot with references to these people and events? ("I don't know" is not an answer, by the way.) What effect is he hoping to have by doing this?

11. Tell about the Green Knight's offer to Arthur's court. Write it up as if you were writing a news story. (Do this on a separate piece of paper. All the usual expectations for neatness and correctness apply.)

DONE!

Gawain and the Green Knight
Worksheet 2

This week you are going to read Book II of *Gawain and the Green Knight* (pages 34-53). Enjoy!

1. Vocabulary

Zephyr	goad (goaded)
linden	stayed (to stay)
wends (to wend)	hewed
*welkin	*barbican
trifling	finials
dint	espy
assayed	blithe
damask	errant
*sabatons	duly
*greaves	stalwart
*cuisses	esquire
*thews	trestles
*byrnie	*surnape
hasp (hasped)	deign
popinjay	hue
blazon	festal
*gules	tryst
baldric	rouse
pentangle	dallied (to dally)
vaunt	bandied (to bandy)
lea	

2. Again, as you did in the last worksheet, record the main characters and events described in each stanza on the chart on the next page. Don't skip this step. Your summary should be very short, more like a title for each stanza than a "book report." If possible, write your titles in you book at the top of each stanza.

3. At what point in the next year does Gawain prepare to leave Camelot to fulfill his promise to the Green Knight?

4. What is that promise, by the way?

5. You will be tempted to skim over stanzas 25-28. Don't. If you didn't look up the vocabulary words before beginning this section, you will be lost, and may skim out of desperation (looking for a familiar word, perhaps). The clothes Gawain puts on are somewhat symbolic. Pay particular attention to the Pentangle.

   You may be familiar with the associations that the pentangle has with regard to witchcraft, and so may be a little put off by its presence here. That is **not** how it is being used in this section.

   The Pentangle is an essentially a five-pointed star. Because it's shape is similar to that of a human body (two legs down, two arms outstretched, head pointed up), in medieval times came to signify the five wounds of Christ. The figure can also be drawn with one stoke, one endless line. Because of this it is also referred to as the "Endless Knot." It was often used as a symbol of Truth.

6. In Stanza 28, what other groups of five are named:

7. What does the pentangle symbolize for Gawain?

8. Describe the hardships faced by Gawain as he traveled.

   "Thus in peril and pain and in passes grievous
       till Christmas-eve that country he crossed all alone in need.
           The knight did at that tide
           his plaint to Mary plead,
           her rider's road to guide
           and to some lodging lead."

   What does Gawain's appeal to Mary tell about him. What is the poet
   trying to tell us about his character? Does Mary answer his
   request?

9. Where does Gawain eventually find refuge? Describe his host and
   hostess.

10. Describe Gawain's relationship with the lady. How does he treat her
    older companion?

11. When Gawain is concerned that he will miss his appointment with the
    big green guy, what does his host promise?

12. Tell about Gawain's relationship with the Lady.

13. Describe their bargain. Tell what each agrees to do?

Stanza	Who?	What?
22		
23		
24		
25		
26		
27		
28		
29		
30		
31		
32		
33		
34		
35		
36		
37		
38		
39		
40		
41		
42		
43		
44		
45		

Gawain and the Green Knight
Worksheet 3

1. Vocabulary: Be able to define the following words correctly.

> abashed
> parley
> constrain
> converse
> demurred
> featly
> averred
> quell

2. Read Book III. As you read each section (see the chart for section divisions), fill out the "Exchange Chart" found on the next page of the worksheet.

Exchange Chart

Stanza	What the Lord caught	What Gawain caught	Other Event/Actions described
46-47			
48-52			
53-56			
57-58			
59-62			
63-67			
68-69			
69-75			
76-77			
78-79			

3. How would you describe the following relationships:

      Gawain and the Lord of the castle

      Gawain and the Lady

      The Lady and the Lord of the Castle:

4. What does the Lady seem to want from Gawain?

5. Why does Gawain not just lock the door, throw her out, stand up in bed and shout, "Away, foul wench!!!"?

6. Does the Host seem to know what his Lady is doing? Does he seem to mind? What do you make of all that?

7. Would you describe Gawain as a faithful knight? Why/why not?

GAWAIN AND THE GREEN KNIGHT
Worksheet 4

1. Read Book IV of Gawain and the Green Knight
   (That includes stanzas 90-101).
   As you read each section continue to fill out the overview chart found
   at the end of this worksheet.

2. What is missing from Gawain's bedroom as he wakes up this last time?
   (Perhaps, I should say WHO is missing?)

3. As his companion leaves him to travel on to the Green Chapel alone,
   what does he try to convince Gawain to do? What promise does he
   make to Gawain?

4. What does Gawain's response tell us about Gawain's character?

5. Describe Gawain's encounter with the Green Knight and his axe. How
   many times does the Green Knight raise his axe? What happens
   each time?

6. Tell the significance of the Green Knight's 'blows." How do they relate to the bargain made by the two men at the castle?

7. When Gawain returns to Camelot, how does he describe his encounter with the Green Knight? What does this tell us about his character?

8. "*Hony soyt qui mal pense*" means, "Shame to him who finds evil here." How does that relate to the poem?

9. Some have described Gawain as a <u>**romantic hero**</u>, while others have said that he is an <u>**epic hero**</u>.

The characteristics of a romance were taken from the article, ***Four Romances of England,*** Edited by Ronald B. Herzman, Graham Drake, and Eve SalisburyOriginally Published in *Four Romances of England,* Kalamazoo, Michigan: Western Michigan University for TEAMS, 1999. They can be found at this internet address, www.lib.rochester.edu/camelot/teams/romint.htm

- focuses more on the personal story of main character less on the national/state

- involves a test or a challenge to test his strength, courage, courtesy (that is, to test the worth of his character)

- usually the challenge involves love. "where in epic, women more usually lure the hero with dilatory lusts, commune weirdly with dead spirits, or stay at home and weave."

- the hero will go through some sort of transformation. He may start off with little promise, but may be transformed into something grand at the end. – "though life starts out hard, by the end the hero is rewarded for perseverance, valor, honor and glory for themselves, wedded bliss, and a restored kingdom to rule."

- hero proves himself through his valor by some test. Usually involves ridding himself of something evil. Romance tends to focus on the <u>individual combat</u> rather than the <u>epic battlefield</u>.

10. List the elements that characterize the epic hero:

11. In the space below list specific things you have noticed from your reading that would support either of these positions:

Gawain is a *Romantic Hero*:

Gawain as an *Epic Hero*:

12. Using your notes (from #11), explain how Gawain is an example of a romantic hero. Use quotations and illustrations from the text. Be logical, concise, and brilliant. No pressure, really.

Stanza	Who are the main people here?	What is the main action/event described?	Comments/observations
80-82			
83-86			
87-88			
89			
90			
91			
92			
93			
94-95			
96-97			
98-99			
100-101			

DONE!

NEXT STOP....CHAUCER!

THE CANTERBURY TALES,
THE PROLOGUE
By Geoffrey Chaucer

For your study of Chaucer, you will be reading the entire *Prologue*, the *Pardoner's Tale* and its *Prologue,* and the *Wife of Bath's Tale* with its *Prologue.*

The Penguin Classic Edition, translated by Neville Coghill is the edition referenced in this study guide.

Historical Background:

Chaucer and His Times:

Middle English:

Before you begin to read the translation of *The Prologue*, go to this website and listen to the Prologue read in Middle English:

http://academics.vmi.edu/english/audio/audio_index.html

The original Middle English text will be displayed on the page as it is read so that you can follow along.

1. LONG-TERM ASSIGNMENTS / MEMORY WORK OPTIONS:

For ONE quiz grade credit: Memorize the first 12 lines in Modern English (you may write this out or recite out loud) or learn to read them (aloud) in Middle English	**For TWO quiz grade credits** Memorize the first 12 lines in Middle English. This one will **have** to be recited orally.

.

The Prologue (in Middle English)

Whan that Aprille, with hise shoures soote,
The droghte of March hath perced to the roote
And bathed every veyne in swich licour,
Of which vertu engendred is the flour;
Whan Zephirus eek with his swete breeth

Inspired hath in every holt and heeth
The tendre croppes, and the yonge sonne
Hath in the Ram his halfe cours yronne,
And smale foweles maken melodye,
That slepen al the nyght with open eye-

So priketh hem Nature in hir corages-
Thanne longen folk to goon on pilgrimages

After we have finished reading the selections in Modern English, I encourage you to go back to this website and listen to at least part of each tale as it is read as Chaucer wrote them. You might follow along in the Modern English as it is read in the Middle English.

2. Now begin your reading of the "Prologue," pages 3-26.
    As you read about each of the pilgrims, fill out the chart found on the next two pages. Note the things you notice about each of them. Chaucer won't directly state, "This man was a vicious, selfish, hypocritical pig." What he will do is imply that the man is a vicious, selfish, hypocritical pig though his description of the man's appearance, behavior, or conversation.

    Read carefully, Be alert to the details Chaucer gives you about each character. He chooses descriptive details very carefully and purposefully. He does not waste words.

CHAUCER'S PILGRIMS
STUDY SHEET (page 1)

Pilgrim	Job Description	Physical Description	Moral Description	Your General Impression
Knight				
Squire				
Yeoman				
Prioress				
Monk				
Friar				
Merchant				
Clerk				
Sergeant				
Franklin				
Haberdasher, Carpenter, Weaver Dyer, Tapestry Maker				
Cook				
Shipman				
Doctor				
Wife of Bath				

CHAUCER'S PILGRIMS
STUDY SHEET (page 2)

Pilgrim	Job Description	Physical Description	Moral Description	Your General Impression
Parson				
Miller				
Manciple				
Reeve				
Summoner				
Pardoner				
"Myself"				
Host				

3. Thinking back over this illustrious group of pilgrims (and using your chart to help you), answer these questions about them. Which of these pilgrims would you

--Want to marry your sister or brother (assuming that you LIKE your sister or brother)?

--Ask to take care of your dog while you go on vacation (assuming that you LIKE your dog)?

--Want for a next-door neighbor?

--Want to party with (assuming that you were planning to party respectably)?

--Want to party with (assuming you were NOT planning to party respectable, which of course is strictly a hypothetical question, since, as we know, you would only party respectably. . .)?

--Buy a car from?

Good work!

THE CANTERBURY TALES,
By Geoffrey Chaucer

THE PARDONER'S PROLOGUE & TALE

At the end of the Physicians Tale, the Pardoner is asked , "Tell us a funny story, break a joke!"

> "Right, by St. Ronyan! but I'll have a soak
> First at this pub. I've got a thirst to slake." ·
> Said he, "I'll drink and eat a bit of cake."
> Outcry arose among the gentlefolk.
> "No, no, don't let him tell a dirty joke!
> Tell something with a moral, something clear
> and profitable, and we'll gladly hear."
> "Granted," he said, "but first I'll have to think;
> I'll ponder something decent while I drink"

This is the immediate context of the first few lines of "The Pardoner's Prologue."

1. Read the first 8 lines of this Prologue.

2. What do you observe about the character of the Pardoner from this?

3. In what way does it confirm or contradict the impression you got of him from his description in the Prologue to the Tales?

4. What is the Pardoner's goal when he preaches?

5. How does use the content of his messages as well as body language to accomplish his goal?

6. If you were playing the role of the Pardoner, how would you deliver the final nine lines of the Prologue?

> But listen, gentlemen; to bring things down
> To a conclusion, would you like a tale?
> Now as I've drunk a draught of corn-ripe ale,
> By God it stands to reason I can strike
> On some good story that you all will like.
> For though I am a wholly vicious man
> Don't think I can't tell moral tales. I can!
> Here' one I often preach when out for winning.
> Now please be quiet. Here is the beginning.

7. Read the Pardoner's Tale.

8. The Pardoner begins to tell the tale of a "company of youngsters" from Flanders, but quickly seems to get sidetracked. The apparent rabbit trail ends at the top of page 250 with the lines, "But sirs, I have a story to relate." What is the point of the rabbit trail? Why does the Pardoner take it? Why do you think Chaucer sends him off on it? What do we learn about our dear Pardoner from this section?

9. What story does the Pardoner tell?

10. In what ways does Chaucer make use of irony in the tale? (Hint: He does so on more than one level.)

11. At the conclusion of his tale, what does the Pardoner do that so upsets the Host?

12. Should you have been sitting right there in the midst of them, whose side would you have taken in this little dispute?

13. In what way is the conflict resolved? (Or do you think it is resolved?)

14. So what do you think of our dear Pardoner now?

THE CANTERBURY TALES,
By Geoffrey Chaucer

THE WIFE OF BATH'S PROLOGUE & TALE

The Wife of Bath's Prologue and Tale have much to say about marriage. It is, in fact one of the tales included in what is known as the "Marriage Group." Observe the details he gives us carefully.

The Wife of Bath's Prologue opens with this,

> "If there were no authority on earth
> Except experience, mine, for what it's worth,
> And that' enough for me, all goes to show
> That marriage is a misery and a woe;"

1. Read the rest of that first paragraph to find how old the good Wife was when she was first married. How many times has she been married?

2. Read from the line "Someone said recently for my persuasion" through the line, "There's a commandment on which I like to dwell."

3. In the chart below, list the Biblical characters she references, and then tell what point she is attempting to illustrate through use of each reference.

Biblical character	Her point?
Jesus	

4. Toward the end of this section, the Wife has much to say on the Church's teaching on marriage or celibacy. What does she say were the current teachings and attitudes about sexuality? What are her thoughts?

5. Make a quick count. How many references to Biblical passages can you find in this section?   What is her take on the matter – who is more virtuous: the wife or the one who chooses never to wed? (from the line beginning "Tell me to what conclusion or in aid" to the line beginning, "There's a commandment on which I like to dwell")

6. Tell about the Wife's husbands. Use the chart below:

Husband #	Old or Young	Good or bad (how so?)	Did she love him? (explain)	Praise/Complaint
1				
2				
3				
4				
5				

7. Why did she love her Johnny?

8. How Biblically literate does the Dame appear to be?

9. Compare her with the other women you met in the Prologue?

On to the Tale….

10. Read the Wife of Bath's Tale, then summarize it below:

11. So, what do women want? (Ladies, is she right?)

12. I'm going to ask you to go below the surface here. Your first reaction to the Dame may be to dismiss her as a bawdy, crude old woman….but I want you to go beyond your first impression.

   In question #9, you were asked to compare her to the other women on the pilgrimage. How does Chaucer portray the "virtuous" women?

13. Other than the obvious "virtue" issues, how does this wife differ from the other female pilgrims?

14. If you have been paying attention so far, you should have noticed that Chaucer likes to indirectly show rather than directly explain his assessment of a pilgrim's character. So what is he trying to communicate about the Wife of Bath?

15. What is he also telling to us about the state of the Church of his day?

You're DONE!

HAMLET ACT I
Worksheet 1

When Shakespeare wrote a play, he assumed that it would be performed. It is, of course, possible to read and understand the plays without seeing them performed, but we miss much of their power if that is our only experience of them. For that reason, it will be good for you to either listen to an audio recording of the play or, even better, to watch a video of *Hamlet* in addition to reading it.

The complete text of *Hamlet* is, by comparison to Shakespeare's other plays, massive. This complete text is rarely performed unedited. In fact, there's some evidence that Shakespeare never performed it all – that the full text is a compilation of all his edits from multiple performances. When the play is performed today, most directors will cut out lines, sections, even whole scenes so that the play will run in the customary two hour timeframe. In order to make sure that all-important information survives the cuts, directors will make other little changes here and there so that everything fits together. Because of this, every production of the play will vary to reflect each directors' interpretation.

Several audio and video productions of the play are available.

The Zeffirelli version, starring Mel Gibson, makes quite a few changes. He cuts scenes, moves lines out of their original location and places them in another scene or Act altogether. He even edits out one of the subplots entirely. (When you read the text of play, you will see several references to a character named Fortinbras, who never appears in the movie.) Even though Zeffirelli does make some significant editorial changes, I recommend that you watch this version of the play. I think it does the best job of capturing the "spirit' of the play (you'll get the pun later, but feel free to laugh now, just to show how smart you are).

Another recent film production of the play (now available on DVD) was directed by Kenneth Branagh. Unlike Zeffirelli, Branagh's goal was to produce an uncut version of the script – nothing was deleted or rearranged. This makes for a VERY long film. Unlike Zeffirelli, who chose to use costumes and sets appropriate to the play's historical setting, Branagh chose to use period costumes and set designs which would place the action in Victorian England. I find that Branagh's production does not wear as well as the Zeffirelli. If you have the time, watch both and see which you like best.

If this is your first study of a Shakespeare play, it may take a while for your ear to adjust to Elizabethan English. If you are used to reading from the King James Version, the language will not seem all too foreign. It will help to listen to an audio production of the play AS YOU READ ALONG. (Do not make the mistake of skipping the reading along part!) Audio productions are readily available through public libraries. Some of the titles can be downloaded to MP3 players or to disc over the internet at no charge. Go to your local public library website for more information about this option.

If you choose to listen to an audio production as you read, I would encourage you to proceed this way:

Read over the section in the study guide pertaining to the day's assignment. Plan to move scene by scene through the study. If you finish reading the scene and cannot answer the questions in the study guide, that is God's way of telling you to read the scene again.

Make sure you know the meanings of the words in the vocabulary list before you start reading.
- Listen to the scene and read along.
- Stop the tape, and fill in the "Hamlet Study Sheet" section for that scene.
- Answer the questions for that scene.
- Start over with the next scene.

Here's how it works: You can't understand the scene if you don't understand the words used in the scene. (Therefore, don't skip the vocabulary assignments) And you won't understand what's happening in the Acts if you don't understand what is happening in the individual scenes. It is easier to re-read a short scene than to have to re-read an entire Act. (Therefore, make sure you understand what is going on in the scene you just read before you go on to the next scene.)

Finally, *whatever you do*, <u>DO NOT</u> make the mistake of thinking you can skip the reading part. (To get the most out of your study of Hamlet, you need to read it for yourself. Trust me.)

VOCABULARY ALERT:
THERE WILL BE LOTS OF VOCABULARY! Look over the word list with highlighter in hand. Mark the words you don't know and look those up. Do this before you start to read the play. (And of course, if you find unfamiliar words as you read that are not on the sacred word list, look those up, too.)

1. **Vocabulary:**

apparition	cariest
fortified	canker
usurp	libertine
avow	dalliance
martial	reek
bode	grapple
eruption	perilous
brazen	breach
ratify	inurned
portentous	sulphurous
privy	enmity
hoard	perturbed
russet	ambiguous
contract	aught
impotent	commend
filial	
jocund	
truant	
gape	
importunity	
circumscribed (not to be	
confused with	
circum*cised*)	
CIRCUM SCRIBED	

2. Put the chart on the next page in front of you as you read *Act I*.
Read *scene i*, and stop.
Fill out the chart for *scene i* only.
          Note who appears in the scene.
          Record the main action, or main event portrayed or described
             in the scene.
          Write down any important lines.
          Write out any questions you might have or comments you
             want to make.
      Then go on to the next scene and do the same things.
      Continue through the play this way.

Hamlet Study Sheet: ACT I

Scene	WHO?	WHAT happens	Important Lines	Questions/comments
i				
ii				
iii				

Scene	WHO?	WHAT happens	Important Lines	Questions/comments
iv				
v				

NOTE: The old King was named Hamlet (he was OLD Hamlet). Young
        Hamlet is his son – and the hero of our play.

3. What is the setting of this first scene? (That is where and when does it
    take place?)

4. What is said about Fortinbras?

5. Tell about the Ghost who appears. What is Bernardo's, Marcellus', and
    Horatio's assessment of the Ghost?

6. Who do they think the Ghost will speak to?

ACT II, scene ii:

7. As the scene opens, Claudius is meeting with two men – Voltemand and
    Cornelius, the Danish ambassadors to Norway. What do you gather
    about the purpose of their meeting?

8. Laertes then asks Claudius for permission to go where?

Why?

What does Claudius say?

9. After this exchange, we meet Hamlet for the first time. What does his relationship with Claudius seem to be?

In Lines 87-117, what does Claudius criticize Hamlet for?

10. Where had Hamlet been studying? What was he studying? Who else is associated with this place, historically speaking?

11. What does Claudius want Hamlet to do?

12. After the King and Queen exit in line 128, Hamlet gives a long speech. Who is he talking to? Who is listening to him?

13. | **When an actor, alone on stage, makes a long speech that only the audience is privy to, that speech is called a soliloquy.**

When a piece of information appears in big, bold type, the wise student will know to pay close attention to that information. The very wise student will memorize the information. And YES, you should learn how to spell "soliloquy."

14. In this SOLILOQUY, what do we learn about Hamlet's feelings about Claudius?

15. Why has Hamlet returned to Denmark? What has happened in his absence? How have things changed?

16. What is your impression of Claudius?

    Laertes?

    Polonius?

    The Queen?

17. What does Hamlet learn from Horatio and friends about the Ghost?

ACT I, scene iii:

18. In this scene, we have a family meeting involving Laertes, Ophelia and Polonius. What is Ophelia's relationship to Hamlet? How do her father and brother feel about this relationship?

19. What does Polonius want Ophelia to do? What is her response?

20. Does this scene change or confirm your earlier impression of Polonius? Explain.

ACT I, scene iv

In this scene Hamlet meets _____ for the first time.

21. What is the mood of this scene as Hamlet waits for the Ghost to appear? How does Shakespeare set the mood?

ACT I, scene vi

22. As the scene opens, who is on stage?

23. What is your impression of the Ghost?

24. How does the Ghost identify himself?   What doubts does Hamlet have
    about his identity?

26. What do you think -- is it an "honest ghost" (or something worse)?

27. What information does the Ghost give Hamlet? What does he want
    Hamlet to do about it?

28. How does the scene end? What do Hamlet and his buddies do?

Reward yourself for your hard work!

HAMLET ACT II
Worksheet 2

1. Vocabulary

prenominate (pre>before/ nominate>named) i.e. named before
taints
bias - (as in, something cut on the bias)
perusal
repel
wrack
foul/ed
adhere
levy/levies
entreaty
expostulate
brevity
maggot
tedious
strumpet
coagulate
carbuncles
repugnant
pate
offal
bawdy

2.   Something you should know:

A **_subplot_** is a literary device used quite frequently by Shakespeare. A
subplot is a secondary story line that will run parallel to the main story.
In Act 2, Shakespeare begins to establish the subplot involving two
fathers and two sons. Watch for this as you read.

3. Read Act 2, Scene I

4. Who talks together as the scene opens?

5. What is Polonius sending his servant off to do?

6. What is your general impression of Polonius?

6. As one character exits, another enters? Who joins Polonius on stage in the second half of the scene? (Give name and relationship, please.)

7. What news does she bring?

8. Explain her relationship to Hamlet.

9. What are your impressions of the following:

    Her relationship with Hamlet –

    Hamlet's true feelings for her –

10. What is your impression of Ophelia?

11. Read Act 2, Scene II.

12. Who enters as the second scene opens?

13. What is the relationship between Hamlet and the following characters –

the King:

the Queen:

Rosencrantz and Guildenstern:

Why has the King summoned them?
What does he want from them?
What exactly does he want to know?

14. Do the King and the Queen seem to be motivated by the same desires? Explain.

15. How does the opening of this scene parallel the opening of the first scene?

16. As Rosencrantz and Guildenstern leave, Polonius enters to announce that the ambassadors from Norway have arrived AND to announce that he KNOWS why Hamlet is not himself. From his first speech to the king here, what can you tell about his character?

17. Voltemand brings news about events in Norway. Apparently the ambassadors have had an earlier audience with the king of Norway in which they expressed concerns about the activities of his young nephew Fortinbras. What did Norway *think* young Fortinbras was raising monies to fund?

What was he really funding?

What did Norway do when he found out the truth?

How did Fortinbras respond to his uncle (according to the ambassadors' report)?

NOTE: Reports of Fortinbras' whereabouts are given here and there throughout the play. Pay attention. The conflict within Denmark between Hamlet and his uncle is set in the context of conflict between Denmark and her neighbors.

18. The ambassadors gone, Claudius and Polonius have much to discuss. Polonius says:

> My liege and madam, to expostulate
> What majesty should be, what duty is,
> Why day is day, night, night, and time is time,
> Were nothing but to waste night, day, and time.
> Therefore, since brevity is the soul of wit,
> And tediousness the limbs and outward flourishes,
> I will be brief. Your noble son is mad.
> Mad call I it, for, to define true madness,
> What is't but to be nothing else but mad?
> But let that go.

What is ironic about the statement, "Since brevity is the soul of wit, . . . I will be brief"?

19. What news does Polonius finally bring to the King and Queen? What do they decide to do with the information?

20. As Hamlet enters reading, the King and Queen exit, leaving who alone with Hamlet?

21. Describe the interaction between Hamlet and Polonious. What does Polonius think about Hamlet? What does Hamlet think about Polonious?

22. You will have noticed this before some characters speak: **[Aside]**

An   **[aside]** is a speech made to the audience as if the actor were drawing *aside* to speak only to the audience outside the hearing of the other actors in the scene.

When Polonius says "Though this be madness, yet there is method in't", what does that tell you about what Polonius believes to be true about Hamlet?

(So, did you notice the bold print?)

23. Is Hamlet oblivious to Polonius' plot or playing with him?

24. As Polonius leaves the stage, who enters?   How does Hamlet receive
        this pair?

25. What does Hamlet attempt to discover about Rosencrantz and
        Guildenstern? What does he learn?

26. When Hamlet says,

    *"Then are our beggars bodies, and our monarchs and
    outstretched heroes the beggar's shadows,"*

    what is he saying about the true nature of monarchs and heroes?
    Make a simple drawing to illustrate his words.

27. Does Hamlet see through Rosencrantz and Guildenstern? How do you
    know?

28. Enter the troupe of traveling actors. Apparently Hamlet has seen this
    troupe before, and likes them very much.   Why are these talented
    performers in the boonies and not still playing in the big city where
    the big money is?

29. What does Hamlet mean by calling the King his "uncle-father" and the
    queen, his "aunt-mother"?

30. How does he say they are deceived?

31. Describe the interaction between Hamlet and Polonius in this scene.

32. Why is Hamlet moved by the Players recitation of the lines which begin, *"Run barefoot up and down, threat'ning the flames.. ."*

33. In Hamlet's closing soliloquy, what does he tell us about himself – his true sense of things?

34. How does he plan to test the truth of the Ghost's accusation and his uncle's innocence or guilt?

FINISHED with ACT II

HAMLET ACT III
Worksheet 3

Welcome to Act III. If you have not read much, or have not made much attempt to increase your vocabulary, you will find LOTS of vocabulary words in this Act. III. Given the number of words, I would recommend working though them scene by scene. That is, look up the words which appear in scene i and then read the scene and answer the questions about this scene. Then look up the words for scene ii and read scene ii and answer the questions. Done before you know it!

Act III, scene i:

1. Vocabulary

niggard

assay

espials (her father and myself, lawful espials) spies

visage

plast'ring art – make-up

consummation

perchance – perhaps

"there's the rub" – impediment

impediment

mortal coil – turmoil of life

turmoil

calamity

contumely

insolence

quietus – acquittance

acquittance

bare bodkin – dagger

fardels –burdens

bourn – boundary

cast (noun) as in "pale cast" (hint: cast does not refer to the troupe of actors)

awry

orison(s)

aught

honest – this is a pun….honest here means both chaste and honest

bawd

pardox

inoculate

arrant

knave

dowry

calumny

wantonness

ecstasy – here means madness

melancholy

hatch and the disclose" when a bird hatches from the egg – *hatch* refers to the breaking of the shell, *disclose* to the emergence of the chick

variable

expel

entreat

"let her be round with him" MEANS let her be direct with him

2. Who enters as this scene opens?

3. What do the king and queen want with Rosencrantz and Guildenstern as the scene opens?

4. Are Ros and Gil able to deliver what Claudius and Gertrude want? Explain.

5. After Ros and Gil leave, the King asks Gertrude to leave. What have he and Polonius devised?

6. How do you think Hamlet would feel about this plan?

7. Hamlet enters talking to himself, seemingly oblivious to all who might or might not be around him. What is it we call a speech given by an actor who appears alone on the stage as he delivers his lines?

8. As Hamlet enters, what is he contemplating? What looks good to him, why?

9. Describe Hamlet's conversation with Ophelia. How would you describe their affections for one another?

10. How does their *audience* interpret what they overhear?

Act III, scene ii:

11. Vocabulary

trippingly
life
groundlings – the part of the
      audience of a play who
      purchase the cheapest
      seats and so stand in the
      open space in front of the
      stage to watch the play.
      The most uneducated and
      unsophisticated members
      of the audience.
judicious
censure
gait
barren
pomp
commingled
occulted
unkennel (to kennel would be to
      keep in a kennel,
      restrained, thus Unkennel
would be to release)
stithy- forge, anvil
Vulcan
censure – to judge
scape – short for escape
chameleon

capons
a suit of sables – a suit of furs, or
      black garments
epitaph
protestation
anon
lament
loath
miching mallecho – skulking
      mischief
skulking
naught
clemency
Hymen
commutual
wormwood
base
validity
enacture – acts
tedious
knavish
galled
pajock – peacock
vouchsafe
choler – anger
purgation

12. Read Act III, scene 1, lines 1-47. Who is on stage at this point?

13. What is Hamlet concerned with in these lines? Why would he be so
      concerned?

14. Read lines 48-91.   Who comes on stage during these lines?

15. What does Hamlet discuss with Horatio?

16. Read lines 92-301.   Who is on stage during this part of the play?   What are they all doing?

17. Describe Hamlet's interaction with Ophelia.   How do his words and actions seem to affect her?

18. Describe the player's play.

19. How does the King react to the play?   How does Hamlet interpret the King's reaction?

20. Read lines 301-407.

21. What message do Rosencrantz and Guildenstern bring to Hamlet?
Describe Hamlet's attitude toward them.

22. What does Hamlet mean when he says, "Will you play upon this pipe?"

23.. The scene closes with a soliloquy. What is the subject of this
soliloquy? Describe Hamlet's thoughts as he goes to meet his
mother.

Act III, scene iii

24. Vocabulary:

annex
annexment
gulf
fetters
arras
convey
*the primal eldest curse upon 't, a
    brother's murder* – what is
    the Biblical reference?
vantage – short for **ad**vantage
liege
rood

penetrable
bulwark
ardor
pander(s)
diadem
incorporeal
conjoined (conjoin'd)
my stern effects – actions
coinage
temperate(ly)
gambol
cleft

25. Read lines 1-35.

26. What does the King tell Rosencrantz and Guildenstern about his plans
    for Hamlet? How do these two dear friends of Hamlet respond to this
    news?

27. Read lines 36-98.

28. Describe the content of the King's prayers.

29. Why doesn't Hamlet kill Claudius while he has the chance? What is a little ironic about his decision not to kill him?

30. Read Scene iv.

31. List the characters appearing in this scene.

32. Tell about Hamlet's conversation with his mother. How does she respond to him?

You've finished ACT III – reward yourself!

HAMLET Act IV
Worksheet 4

Act IV, scenes i, ii, and iii

Vocabulary

pith
as the cannon to his blank – the blank refers to the white center of the target.
replication – in this case, means *reply*
a progress – a royal journey made by a king and his attendants
convocation

1. Read Scenes 1 to 3.

2. What can you tell from the King's soliloquy at the beginning of scene 3 about his intentions toward Hamlet?

Act IV, scene iv

Vocabulary

Before you read the scene, read through the vocabulary glosses in the margin of your text. There are many obsolete and just plain obscure words and phrases in this section. Note them before you read the scene, and it will be less confusing.

3. .As the scene opens, Hamlet happens upon Fortinbras' army and asks one of the officers about their intent. Does he seem to realize that Fortinbras intends to attack Denmark?

4..What is the point of Hamlet's soliloquy at the end of this scene? What is
    he musing over?

5. Compare Hamlet's behavior in the last scene with his behavior in this
    scene. How sane or crazy does he appear to really be? Why would
    he pretend to be crazy?

Scenes v and vi

Vocabulary

superfluous
ratify (does not have anything to do with large rodents)
ratifiers

6. Read Scene 5.

7. What has happened to Ophelia? What is the tone of this scene?

8. As Laertes enters, what is his mood? What does he demand of
    Claudius? How does Claudius respond to him?

9. .Read Scene 6.

10.Such a short scene! Horatio receives a letter. Who is it from and what
    does it say?

What do we learn about Hamlet from the letter? Is Claudius' plan
going well?

Scene vii

Vocabulary

acquittance (root word is *aquit*)
peruse
contagion
"if I gall him slightly"

11. Read Scene vii.

12. Describe Claudius' relationship with Laertes. Why is Laertes so buddy-buddy with the King?

13. When Claudius gets word that Hamlet will in fact return, what new plan does he hatch with Laertes?   Why is Laertes so willing to do Claudius' dirty work for him?

14. When the Queen says, "One woe doth tread upon another heel. So fast they follow," to what is she referring?

15. As Laertes leaves the stage, Claudius says to Gertrude,

> How much I had to do to calm his rage!
> Now fear I this will give it start again"

How much *has* Claudius done to calm Laertes' rage? What does this comment tell us about Claudius?

16. Knowing what you know so far, how truthful does the Ghost's accusations against Claudius appear to be? What kind of man is Claudius? Cite specific examples from the play to support your answer. I need evidence, dear Watson, evidence! (a little Sherlock Holmes allusion there......)

17. How would you describe the mood as Act IV closes?

And the curtain falls on Act IV! APPLAUSE!

HAMLET Act V
Worksheet 5

Scene i

1. **Vocabulary**

wittingly

In Shakespeare's time the cheapest tickets would have cost one penny, which would have actually been a full day's wages. These tickets bought a person a space to stand on the ground at the foot of the stage – hence they were called *groundlings*. Obviously if you could afford a better ticket you would buy one that would allow you to sit and watch the play. The poorer, less educated playgoers would fill the area in front of the stage, and Shakespeare often wrote scenes with them in mind. These tended to be the comic, often bawdy scenes. These clowns, appearing as the gravediggers, would have appealed to the groundlings.

2. Read Act V, scene i. Note: It is worth watching the gravedigger's scene in Branagh's Hamlet, even if you do not watch his entire show, for two reasons. First, Branagh cast Billy Crystal as the gravedigger – a perfect match of actor and role. Second, Branagh films the entire unedited text of the scene – the scene is almost always cut short and the lines are some of Shakespeare's most powerful. You may be able to find a five minute clip of this scene on YouTube. Watch it if you can.

3. What is the tone of the opening scene of Act V? Compare it with the tone of the closing scene of Act IV.

4. What information do we learn from the gravediggers?

5. As Hamlet comes on the scene, what does he not know that the gravediggers and the audience do know?

6. Who was Yorick? How was he significant to Hamlet?

7. What is the point of this soliloquy? ('*Your guess is as good as mine*," is really not the best answer. Try again.)

8. As Hamlet realizes that Ophelia is the one being buried, how does he respond?

9. How does Laertes respond to Hamlet?

10. If you hadn't eavesdropped on Claudius' conversation with Laertes in the previous Act, how would you interpret his attitude toward Hamlet?

11. What does his conversation with Laertes at the end of the scene tell you about Claudius?

12. How did Hamlet feel about Ophelia?

Scene ii

In the last Act, Laertes received a letter from Hamlet letting him know that he would be home soon. In this scene, Hamlet gives Laertes the full report of his little voyage.

13. Read Scene ii.

14. In lines 4-24, what does Hamlet describe doing?

15. What did the letter specifically commission (or command)?

16. How did Hamlet's "new commission" change things around?

17. Describe the messenger, Osric. What does Hamlet think of him? (How can you tell?)

18. What does message does Osric bring?

19. And what message does the Lord (who enters after line 196) bring?

20. Does Hamlet accept the wager?

21. If you were playing Horatio, how would you play this scene? What would you be feeling? What would you want to communicate to your audience?

22. How does Hamlet take Horatio's advice?

23. Describe the trap Claudius has set for Hamlet?

24. If you were playing Laertes in this scene. How would you play it? Would your attitude toward Hamlet remain the same throughout the scene? (Explain, please.)

25. Tell about Hamlet's opening words to Laertes. How do you react to
     them? Does he appear to be sincere? How does Laertes respond?

26. How does the Queen's drinking to Hamlet's victory spoil the King's well
     laid out plan?

27. When Gertrude falls, what light begins to dawn on yon young Hamlet?
     (a little Shakespeare lingo, there. . .)

28. Tell who dies, in what order they die, and how they die. (This is a
     tragedy after all.)

29. What two groups arrive on the scene after Hamlet's death? What do each come expecting?

30. Why did Fortinbras come? How does he respond to the scene before him?

31. Take a break of at least a day. (Hope you're not reading this for the first time the night before class!) Think about the play, about Hamlet and all he has been through. The play is called a *tragedy*. How is it tragic?

32. A tragic hero is defined as a good man who is brought to ruin by means of some flaw in his character. What would Hamlet's tragic flaw be?

33. A recurring theme in the Shakespeare's plays has to do with the proper order of things. When all things are properly aligned – spiritually, nationally, personally – there is a right order within a kingdom. One area can not be out of alignment without affecting all the others. How does Shakespeare develop this theme in *Hamlet*?

34. So was the ghost a demon from hell, or a true ghost? (Explain your answer.)

35. What other things did you notice in the play that you would like to discuss?

36. Oh MY! It has just occurred to me that questions 32, or 33, or even 34, could make very good essay topics! Because you are good students, I know you've already put much thought and energy into answering them. And because you are such dedicated students, I know you won't be satisfied until you have fully answered them. So choose which one (#32, 33, or 34) you would like to write a 2-3 page essay on. As usual, support you position by quoting actual passages from the actual play. Have fun.

Good job!! You are done. You have finished your study of *Hamlet*.
Treat yourself to something special
before leaping from Shakespearean tragedy into existential angst!
Then on to *Rosencrantz and Guildenstern Are Dead!*

LESSON 20

Background for
Rosencrantz and Guildenstern Are Dead!
By Tom Stoppard

Existentialism

With *Hamlet* we have completed our chronological study of Medieval (and this part of our study of Renaissance) English Literature. Now for something a little different.

You have been reading material that has about it a common world view. From Bede through Shakespeare the writers you have read so far in this course have assumed that some things were true about the world. On the chart found on the next two pages, summarize the beliefs about each of the things listed there under "Medieval World View," then note whether those things change or remain constant in *Hamlet*.

With *Rosencrantz and Guildenstern are Dead!* we are about to switch gears. The play in an example of what is called, Theater of the Absurd – a theatrical expression of existentialism. *Ros & Gil* is based on Shakespeare's *Hamlet*, but Stoppard's philosophical perspective is radically different from Shakespeare's. In studying this play, we have an opportunity to see what a difference a shift in worldview can make. In preparation for reading the play, you also need to do a little research on Existentialism. Here are a few web addresses to get you started:

http://www.thecry.com/existentialism/ (general summary)
http://www.anselm.edu/homepage/dbanach/sartreol.htm
(another excellent summary)
http://www.marxists.org/reference/archive/sartre/works/exist/sartre.htm
(an essay by Jean Paul Sartre, one of the leading existential philosophers)

As you do your research, fill out the final column of the chart under the heading, *Existentialism*.

	MEDIEVAL WORLD VIEW	HAMLET	EXISTENTIALISM
God's character: What is He like? (is He seen as a He?)			
Is there a single deity or multiple deities?			
What is God's relationship with Man?			
What kind of relationship does He desire to have with Man?			
Does he care what happens to Man and if he cares, how would you know it?			
Man's nature: What is Man? Where does he come from? What is he like? What is his relationship like with God? With other men? How does he see himself?			

That's all for now. Next step is to read *Ros and Gil* for yourself. If you can find someone to read it aloud with, so much the better. A good time will be had by all.

Rosencrantz and Guildenstern Are Dead!
ACT 1
Worksheet 2

1. After reading through the play, you have, no doubt, noticed some striking references to Shakespeare's *Hamlet*.
   This week I want you to go back and dig into it.

2. *Rosencrantz and Guildenstern Are Dead!* is divided into three acts:
   Act 1: pages 11-54
   Act 2: pages 55-95
   Act 3: pages 96-126

   This week you are going to concentrate only on Act 1.

   Stoppard does not break the play down into individual scenes, but Act I can be divided up into the following segments:

pp. 11-21	The coin toss and toss and toss and toss….
pp 21- 34	The players
pp.34- 37	Enter Ophelia, Claudius, Gertrude, et al.
bottom of 37-52	Analysis/Question Game
52-53	Enter Hamlet

3. Describe the coin tossing sequence. Why is the outcome odd, and how do Ros and Gil account for its oddness?

4. What are Ros and Gil trying to figure out in Act 1?

5. What do they know? (List)

6. What don't they know? (List)

7. What is the significance of Gil's unicorn speech on pp. 21?

8. Mark the following key words in a distinctive way. (You are going to mark
   them all the way through the play.)

   remember (and any synonyms)
   forgetting (and any synonyms)

9. Some things to ponder (would be a good idea to jot down some notes, too):

- The Player's comments about entrances and being "in character' and 'in costume "

- The Player's comments about his craft.

- The significance of the Player (and poor Alfred)

- The significance of the coin toss

- The significance of the question game

- Hamlet's greeting of Ros and Gil -- or is it Gil and Ros?

- Other things that struck you.

- Also, be on the lookout for lines and images that echo lines and images and themes found in *Hamlet*. They will begin to jump out at you. Mark them when you see them.

10. I'm sure that by now you have an opinion as to the moral character of the Player. How would you describe the dear man?

Enough fun for one week.

Rosencrantz and Guildenstern Are Dead
ACT 2
Worksheet 3

The Player: "We keep to our usual stuff, more or less, only inside out. We do onstage the things that are supposed to happen off. Which is a kind of integrity, if you look on every exit being an entrance somewhere else."

1. Act 2 can be divided into the following segments:

    1. pages 55-56 – This conversation between Ros and Gil and Polonius and Hamlet which is the set up for the second segment on …
    2. pages 56-61   -- the Question Game and their attempt to understand what has happened between the four of them.
    3. pages 61-72 -- Polonius, Hamlet, and Player exit, and Ros and Gil continue to analyze through page 72
    4. pages 72-81 –   "The play's the thing!"
    5. pages 82-95 – The spies / England

2. Continue to mark all references to *memory, remembrance, remember.* List the things they can remember.

    Also, mark all references to *death*.

    And mark all references to *know* (both negative and positive).

3. What seems to be the significance of the Question Game? What does it tell you about Ros and Gil?

4. Read the section that begins of page 70 with "Do you ever think of yourself as dead, actually lying in a box with a lid on it?" and ends with "Death followed by eternity, the worst of both worlds" on page 72.

   Read carefully, what is Stoppard's point here? What are Ros and Gil saying about life now and life after death? What are they sure of? What are not sure of?

5. Why is Ros near tears mid-page 75?

6. How does Stoppard's player's production (the play-within-the-play) differ from the play Shakespeare's players put on?

7. How do those changes affect meaning? Or, how does Shakespeare's "play" move the story forward? Compare/contrast with the "play" in Ros & Gil.

8. What troubles Ros & Gil about the Spies? What do they appear to represent?

9. Comment on the references to *death* in this Act.

10. What do Ros & Gil know? What do they want to know? What don't they know?

11. Note the references to music in Acts 1 and 2. What seems to follow those references? What does music seem to represent for Ros and Gil?

12. Describe the mood at the end of Act 2? How has the mood changed? What contributes to the change, or how does Stoppard make you *feel* that change?

ROSENCRANTZ AND GUIDENSTERN ARE DEAD! ACT 3
Worksheet 4

1. Just to recap: at the end of Act 2, for the first time in the play, what happened?

2. At the beginning of Act 3, where are Ros and Gil (or is it Gil and Ros)? If you were in the audience, what would the stage look like throughout the first part of the scene?

3. What are Ros and Gil afraid the darkness means for them?

4. Even though the scene is very funny, what very **not** funny things run right below the surface of it all?

5. As the light comes up, what things become visible to the audience? What does the audience become aware of?

6. As you read this Act, pay attention to the comments about boats. When you are done reading Act 3, come back and tell what symbolic significance *boats* have here. You might specifically note Guil's comments on the topic (below), and the Player's comment as he emerges from the barrel: "Aha! All in the same boat then!" (Act 3, page 114)

GUIL: "Yes, I'm very fond of boats myself. I like the way they're – contained. You don't have to worry about which way to go, or whether to go at all – the question doesn't arise, because you're on a *boat*, aren't you? Boats are safe areas in the game of tag. . .the players will hold their positions until the music starts. . . I think I'll spend most of my life on boats. . . "

GUIL: "Free to move, speak, extemporize, and yet. We have not been cut loose. Our truancy is defined by one fixed star, and our drift represents merely a slight change of angle to it: we may seize the moment, toss it around while the moments pass, a short dash here, an exploration there, but we are brought round full circle to face again the single immutable fact – that we, Rosencrantz and Guildenstern, bearing a letter from one king to another are taking Hamlet to England." (Act 3, pages 100-101)

7. Also, pay attention to the significance of the letter. Mark references to it as you read. Describe Ros and Gil's attitudes toward the letter. What importance do they attach to it (and why)?

8. When Ros and Gil read the first letter, how do they respond to the contents?

Does knowing what it says change their actions at all? What does that tell about their characters? (Dig deep here....)

9. As the player and his troupe reappear, how are they dressed? Why are they dressed this way? How does Stoppard make use of this as the play ends?

10. Note the references to death as the play draws to an end. Mark them.

11. After you have finished the play come back to the references to death you've marked. What do you *glean*?

12. What do Ros and Gil sense about the way things seem to be headed? What is the role of the players in this?

13. After Ros and Gil disappear, what scene from Hamlet re-emerges?

14. So, what is the point? What does the play have to say about life and purpose, fate, death?

15. List (this maybe repetitive, but do it anyway) the things that Ros and Gil KNOW.

16. Now, list the things Ros and Gil do NOT know.

17. What are the larger implications of each of those things?

18. What is Stoppard suggesting about the nature/state of modern man?
    What do we know?
    What don't we know?
    Is there a Higher, Ordering Power?
    A Personal, Caring God?
    Describe the universe assumed in the play.

19. Take each of the points you noted in 15-18 and think about what the Gospel has to say to each one. Think beyond the easy religious answers that are easy to write down, think about what these answers really would mean to the "Ros and Guils" around us.
    What a good essay topic this would be!

    Write an essay in which you skillfully develop your thoughts into a stunning written argument.

20. Once you have finished your essay, you will have completed your work for this course. Good job! Though I know it is a bittersweet thing to be done forever with this study, I'm sure you will find ways to cope.

Printed in the United States
122701LV00001B/47-70/P

9 781882 514458